GYMNASTIC SKILLS

GYMNASTIC SKILLS

The Theory and Practice of Teaching and Coaching

ROGER MACE
MA, LCP, DipPhys Ed (Carnegie), Teachers Cert (Loughborough)

BARRY BENN
DLC, DipPhys Ed (Leeds)
National Coach to English Schools Gymnastics Association
National Coach to British Amateur Gymnastics Association

BATSFORD ACADEMIC AND EDUCATIONAL LTD
LONDON

Printed and bound in Great Britain by
R. J. Acford Ltd., Industrial Estate, Chichester, Sussex

for the publishers
Batsford Academic and Educational Ltd
4 Fitzhardinge Street
London W1H 0AH

ISBN 0 7134 4307 3 (boards)

Contents

PREFACE

Planning the Programme, published in 1952, was the last Ministry publication which gave practical guidance to teachers on the teaching of gymnastics. The intervening 30 years have seen a revolution in the approach to gymnastics, the pre-specified objectives model of the curriculum being replaced by an open-ended process model which has been accompanied by a plethora of books exhorting this approach. Over recent years this latter model has been seriously questioned when applied to physical skill teaching. As with many revolutions, all that is good in the old is discarded for no better reason than that it was part of that which existed. However, recent curriculum investigations have shown that the process model has distinct limitations, whilst one of the outcomes of this approach has been the almost total annihilation of secondary boys' gymnastics.

This book, written by a practising teacher and a college lecturer, aims to redress the balance. Far from merely recalling a former stereotyped methodology, it takes an eclectic approach but with a bias towards a pre-specified objectives model.

It is written with the practising class teacher very much in mind, and it spells out clearly the need for physical preparation, how individual differences can be accommodated and how certain core skills, basic to gymnastics, should be taught in a class situation. Although the approach is primarily a practical one, the authors have not neglected the theory on which their approach is based.

I welcome this book as I hope will all teachers of boys' gymnastics since it not only answers the constant plea of class teachers for guidance but will do much to put the teaching of secondary boys' gymnastics back in its rightful place on the curriculum.

Chichester 1982   R. Garner
County Physical Education Adviser,
Sussex
Chairman of English Schools
Gymnastic Association

ACKNOWLEDGMENT

We would like to express our thanks to the many colleagues and friends who have given us support and encouragement throughout the preparation of this book. We are particularly indebted to John White who spent many hours carefully studying the text. We are also grateful to Charles Burnup, Rod Lumley, Ian Cockerill, Colin Jewitt, Martin O'Leary, Bede Redican and Anne Wheelhouse for their valuable comments and advice. Finally our thanks to David Barlow for his cartoons and to Julie Watkins for typing the manuscript.

Birmingham 1982   Roger Mace
Barry Benn

FOREWORD

During the last 30 or 40 years Gymnastics has become a central and often controversial issue within the physical education curriculum. At all official levels, in other words, in schemes of work, college courses, DES and LEA publications it has been seen as a core element in the subject at all ages and for both sexes. Without doubt the major impetus in that time came from the introduction of Modern Educational Gymnastics and, in due course, its many derivatives. At the same time traditional gymnastics, relying mainly upon vaulting and agility, never died. Perhaps the most powerful influence of the new work was its application of individualised learning to the teaching of gymnastic movement. Basic elements were defined and the process of learning and the fulfilment of potential were crucial. Traditionalists still leaned heavily upon progressive practices leading to a series of defined goals. At about the same time competitive gymnasts began to realise that stereotyped movements were limiting and sought greater and more diverse ranges of movement. The sport of competitive gymnastics has become well established, especially amongst the young, and is spilling over into school clubs and lessons. Unfortunately, a number of teachers have fallen between stools and confused the aims of Modern Educational Gymnastics with those of traditional work.

The two authors are both educators of considerable experience and by a combination of two major areas of study have re-examined an approach to gymnastics. Roger Mace is a Senior Lecturer in Physical Education with a special interest in the psychology of skill learning and Barry Benn is a Head of Department at the Birmingham Athletic Institute and an internationally known gymnastics coach.

Chapters One and Two outline the elements involved in the teaching and practice of gymnastics and are basic reading for coaches, teachers and performers. The authors' approach is towards the traditional end of the spectrum and they are clearly committed to gymnastics with known end products in terms of defined skills. The objectives are defined and the structure of the tuition leads in those directions. They have, however, been influenced by the concept of individualised learning so that throughout the text they allow for differences and offer flexibility in approach and end result that go a long way towards making the case for individual approach to traditional gymnastics.

Their attention to safety is important, as their methods, though child centred, are to a large degree teacher-directed. They clearly hope to help pupils and students to enjoy gymnastics to the full by ensuring that each pupil in a class will have a target to achieve that is within his/her grasp.

Chapter Three examines the aims and objectives and sets out the what it is the authors hope to achieve by their approach. Having clearly defined their objectives they do not set out to denigrate other approaches but simply to offer to the many teachers who feel best suited to teaching traditional gymnastics a plan and structure that will lead to enjoyment and success by pupils and professional gratification to teachers.

Chapter Four deals in simple terms with the complex issues involved in theoretical aspects of teaching and learning motor-skills, and will be of particular interest to students, teachers and coaches who wish to know more about the process of skill learning.

Chapter Five on Motivation, Emotion and Fear in Gymnastics is an analysis of theories in these areas. Students, teachers and coaches must consider these factors and to dismiss under-performance as simply being 'all in the mind' indicates a failure to understand how learning and performance by gymnasts are influenced by non-physical components which are as much the concern of the teacher or coach as are the more tangible components of skill.

In summary, I recommend all those interested in gymnastics to read the direct practical and down to earth guidance on teaching gymnastics in the early part of the book. The later chapters of the book will be of special interest to teachers and coaches who need to understand how physical skill is learned. To newcomers it provides an introduction to the complex area of the psychology of learning and to experienced tutors it will serve to remind them of the nature of their task.

Birmingham 1982   Charles Burnup
Staff Inspector for Physical Education
City of Birmingham

INTRODUCTION

During the past few years children of all ages have shown an increasing interest in gymnastic skills. This book makes no attempt to analyse reasons for this surge of interest but there can be little doubt that television coverage of Olympic gymnastics and the impact of personalities such as Olga Korbut, Nadia Comaneci, Nikolai Andrianov and Nellie Kim has been particularly significant. Whatever the reasons, an increasing interest is evident and many physical education teachers in schools throughout the country are beginning to reappraise the role and contribution of traditional gymnastics to the school curriculum. It is rare that curriculum change is brought about by the demands of children in the school but it is possible that this is happening. The number of teachers using the British Amateur Gymnastic Association (BAGA) Award Scheme skills as lesson material will verify this. It is our contention that while the Award Scheme skills are most valuable for their original purpose they are inadequate to form the basis of lesson material for a large class within which there is a wide range of ability.

One of the aims of this book is to present numerous skills mainly at a basic level which we hope physical education teachers will find valuable in the preparation of gymnastics lessons. The emphasis in this context lies on the development of specific skills. The named skills associated with traditional gymnastics have evolved through a gradual expansion of experience and understanding of technique by coaches and performers who have distilled the essence from families of skills such as the Kip action into isolated, defined and specific skills. These skills, such as the headspring, are then taken as the basis for variation in much the same way as the educational approach. Thus understanding and proficiency in the basic named skills gives a sound base from which development and exploration can proceed. We are also of the opinion that children who have experienced a number of years of the educational approach should have little difficulty in learning many of the specific skills.

Many teachers feel that while traditional gymnastics is a worthwhile leisure pursuit and club activity, it is not a suitable subject for lessons where the teacher has to cope with a wide range of ability. We do not share this view. It appears to us that lesson material of worthwhile and valuable nature is often not being taught because of failure to develop a teaching method which caters for 'fat Johnny' and 'tall Sally'. Accordingly, one of our aims is to outline an approach to teaching which caters for a range of ability. Basically our problem is no different from that of the mathematics teacher taking a mixed ability class. One of the reasons for the virtual abandonment during the last fifteen years of the teaching of specific 'traditional' gymnastic skills, such as headsprings and handsprings, was because of problems associated with teaching mixed ability groups. It is ironic that few teachers questioned the value of teaching specific games skills, such as the lay-up shot in basketball, to a class of mixed ability.

Physical education teachers find that the teaching of specific skills may be both rewarding and frustrating, we believe that a knowledge of how people become more skilful is important if a successful teaching method is to be developed. Discoveries in motor learning and human performance are helping us to gain a deeper understanding of the learning of motor skills. Consequently, we have included sections on the acquisition of gymnastic skills and on motivation in the hope that the teacher will gain more insight into the factors which influence the learning and performance of these skills.

Birmingham 1982 RM and BB

CHAPTER ONE

Teaching gymnastic skills

Teaching strategies for physical education have varied during the last 50 years. The traditional 'command' method was gradually replaced by a technique which sought to inspire learning through a problem solving approach. In 1963 Bilborough and Jones wrote;

> . . . 'the whole purpose of recent changes is lost if the traditional command-response method of instruction alone is used. The first essential of the teacher of physical education is to adopt a much more natural and conversational manner than was used previously and to speak to the children in the same way as in any other lesson. Formal 'drill' commands should be discarded in favour of a more informal approach.' (p. 28.)

Although written for the primary school teacher, the views expressed in their book were to have a considerable influence on teaching methods in secondary schools. However, by 1973 the pendulum had started to swing back and the same authors wrote;

> 'In both education and physical education this period (1945–1973) has seen extreme formality and teacher dominance on the one hand and extreme informality on the other. During the last few years these extremes have come closer together.' (Bilborough, A, Jones, P 1973:17.)

In recent years some experts on educational curricula have made a plea for a return to traditional teaching methods. The question facing teachers today is which method is more effective for the teaching of physical education, for example, a problem solving approach or a direct more formal approach. Unfortunately this is a question which cannot currently be resolved. Indeed it may never be resolved if the problem is approached in an over-simplified and generalised manner.

It is possible that teachers can come nearer to a solution if they examine closely their aims and objectives. If one of the aims is to help children develop co-operation or reasoning in games situations, it is possible that a structured problem-solving approach incorporating a guided discovery teaching method may be most beneficial. The teacher of traditional gymnastic skills, however, is essentially concerned with helping children to develop a particular response which is performed in a relatively stable environment. Initially, at least, the development of such aspects as creativeness and ingenuity plays a relatively unimportant part. The encouragement and development of these aspects may be considered later when a child is able to perform a wide range of basic skills. He may, for example, be asked to develop a floor routine incorporating a jump into place, a spring and a balance and show good linking moves.

In order to help children acquire the basic gymnastic skills the teacher should aim to direct attention to specific movement patterns with emphasis being laid on style, form and technique. Unlike in the games situation there is relatively little danger that a fixed habitual response will inhibit and detract from performance at a later stage. However, such is the specific nature of skill that a handspring leading to a front somersault may be considered as a separate skill from a handspring which is to terminate in a standing position.

The approach to teaching gymnastics outlined in this chapter is based on the assumption that one of the aims of a teacher is to help children to acquire specific gymnastic skills as, for example, forward roll straddle, rear vault, handstand and forward roll. If this is to be the aim then a successful teaching method must overcome the many difficulties associated with teaching a class of mixed ability. These difficulties must not be underrated. Individuals in a class will vary considerably in size, ability, backround experiences, flexibility and strength. All these have to be taken into account when the teacher sets out to develop specific skills. It is probably true to say that these difficulties have caused a number of teachers to abandon traditional gymnastic skills teaching. This, plus the displacement of traditional gymnastics in favour of educational gymnastics in many colleges of education during the last 15 years, has resulted in the virtual disappearance of traditional gymnastics from the curriculum. Many teachers today teach educational gymnastics convinced that it is the only form of gymnastics suitable for lesson material. If they teach traditional gymnastics at all it is as a club activity after school where only the more able pupils attend.

In view of the considerable value of traditional gymnastics as a vehicle for the broader aims and objectives of physical education the abandonment of the teaching of specific skills is clearly undesirable. Unfortunately relatively few teachers are being trained to teach traditional gymnastics to classes of mixed ability. There are numerous courses on coaching or on the BAGA Award Scheme but the content of these courses is not designed to meet the needs of a class teacher of physical education. The Award Scheme has considerable merit but the content provides insufficient lesson material.

It is perhaps pertinent to point out at this stage that the teaching strategy proposed has been devised for teachers of pupils in their middle years of schooling. However, this does not preclude teachers of younger or older children from using this approach. Although the relationship between stages of motor development and the acquisition of sports skills is possibly less well researched than other areas of study, it does seem likely that specific instruction of children at this early age is likely to have a positive effect on basic and purportedly naturally acquired skills (Cratty 1975:147).

Children want to acquire skill in a wide range of activities. When a child learns a new skill the success and pleasure he feels is apparent. 'Please Sir I can do it ... watch' can be frequently heard in a good gymnastics skills lesson. Hopefully this book will assist teachers by providing a guide so that children are able to enjoy a wide range of gymnastic skills and experiences. It may well be that such experiences will assist in developing a positive attitude to gymnastics and, hopefully, towards physical education in general.

It is inevitable that the content and teaching method outlined will be compared to educational gymnastics. We make no attempt to discuss the relative value of these two different forms of teaching gymnastics. What we offer is a

'Mixed ability is normally a problem for a teacher but since you are all of the same ability, today we will do handsprings'

method of teaching traditional gymnastic skills to mixed ability groups which teachers may adopt or reject according to their philosophy. There are occasions when a knowledge of educational gymnastics methods may be of value in a traditional gymnastics lesson. It is perhaps unwise, however, to encourage the student teacher to combine both approaches. On many occasions these two forms of gymnastics have differing aims and objectives and a student may become confused in his approach leading to a lack of success. In order to combine both approaches a teacher needs to be very clear on his aims and possess a wide content knowledge of educational gymnastics tasks and specific traditional gymnastic skills.

In the 1960s a marked polarisation occured between these two approaches to the teaching of gymnastics. Both approaches have their advantages and disadvantages. In educational gymnastics, novice teachers are faced with problems of communicating concepts to children, such as transference of weight. In traditional gymnastics a teacher is faced with the problem of individual progress and development while teaching skills directly to a class of mixed ability. (See cartoon opposite.)

The views expressed above on teaching gymnastic skills are largely endorsed by Willee (1978). In a paper on *directive* and *non-directive* teaching methods he points out that while the advantages claimed for non-directive methods are well documented by respected authorities it is unfortunate that with the passage of time

others have come to hail non-directive methods as the only approach. This is certainly true for the teaching of gymnastics in this country. Many schools have adopted the non-directive method associated with the teaching of educational gymnastics to the exclusion of direct teaching of specific skills. Willee also referred to the belief that directed discovery methods avoid the failure sometimes experienced under more formal methods. He suggested that directive methods do not have any more inbuilt failures than directed discovery methods with regard to preventing a child from knowing that he is inferior to others in the class.

'Presented with the task of getting from one side of the box horse to another, children who can but walk around would not be unaware that the child who ran and jumped and performed a two and a half front somersault with full twist over the box was in some respects superior.' (p.25.)

The authors are in sympathy both with this view and the child who lands after completing a two and a half front somersault! (See below.)

The essence of the teaching method for the development of specific traditional gymnastic skill is a direct formal approach used to develop specific movement responses. However, unlike the rigid direct methods used some years ago, we are suggesting a more flexible approach to cater for a wide range of ability. This approach is possible only if the teacher possesses an in depth knowledge of 'core skills' and the numerous variations possible based on each of these skills. The

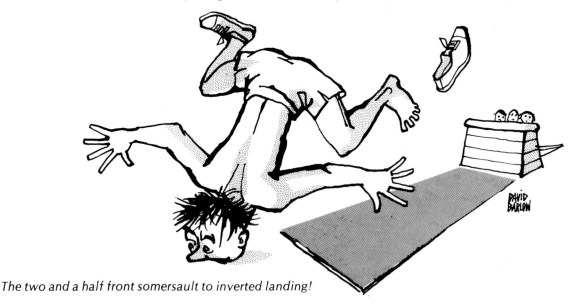

The two and a half front somersault to inverted landing!

rationale behind the teaching manner is based on psychological aspects of skills acquisition. Although in this chapter reference is made to certain theoretical concepts as, for example, reinforcement or information overload, they do not form the central core of the text. However, an understanding of the application of learning theories and of the importance of motivation can help the teacher in the presentation of his content. Accordingly, these aspects are discussed in later chapters.

Core skills

Fundamental to the teaching strategy outlined below is the selection of *core skills*. Examples are, forward roll, backward roll, handstand, straddle vault. These skills are introduced to the class using a direct approach. Consequently there is often a class activity time, usually at the beginning of the lesson, immediately after the warm up activities, when the teacher introduces the core skill. He should aim to help children acquire the skill by developing an efficient movement pattern at the outset. In the forward roll for example, attention should be paid to hand positioning and a tight curled position with weight going from hands onto shoulders. As there is usually a wide range of ability within a class the time spent on class activity time should be relatively short. Class activity work has been criticised on the grounds that pupils of mixed ability are working on the same skill. However, in actual practice the range of ability manifests itself in varying levels of performance. Accordingly, this is a period of time when the teacher should encourage perfection in those who can immediately perform the core skill as well as helping others acquire the basic movement pattern. The approach should be flexible rather than dogmatic and the teacher should encourage repetition to improve quality of performance. As a child learns a skill there is usually a lack of quality in the initial stages. Teachers should therefore be able to analyse performances carefully and help children develop good style and technique. Positive habits should be developed as early as possible, incorrect responses acquired in early stages of learning are difficult to eradicate at a later date. Further there is a tendency for bad habits to re-occur during periods of stress, as for example in competition, long after the teacher believes he has changed the original poor movement pattern.

Teaching skills

It is important to point out that teaching strategies should take into account the previous experience of the children. Consequently it is perhaps best to consider two strategies (a) one suitable for introducing and developing a wide range of core skills and (b) one suitable for introducing moves which are suitable for a specific group within a class. The former concentrates on a certain amount of *class activity* teaching where a particular skill is introduced to the whole class. The second method may be used to help individuals improve their range of skills and is possibly more appropriate when a wide range of core skills has been acquired. This method may involve group organisation on an ability basis. It may also be used however for introducing a core skill for which there is limited apparatus, eg, one set of beams. The class is organised into groups and rotate around various pieces of apparatus but the teacher stays at the beam helping boys develop a particular skill.

Introducing core skills and their variations

It is not sufficient simply to introduce and help develop a range of *core skills* on their own. Various stages should be used to ensure that the children have background experiences in moves which will assist in the acquisition of a particular skill. Also, because of the wide range of ability and consequent different rates of learning, a teacher must be prepared to suggest variations in the skill so that each child is working at a suitable level. The stages which a teacher may use are

1 Introducing skills
2 Orientation activities
3 Class activity on a core skill
4 Skill expansion
5 Variations
6 Sequences

Whilst the various stages have been individually indicated it should be clear that stages could be ignored or merged where appropriate. The nature of the skill and ability of the children are obviously important considerations.

1 Introducing skills

Prior to the introduction of the core skill the teacher should give consideration to the selection and use of warm up activities. Traditionally, the inclusion of such activities has been based on the grounds of a beneficial physiological and psychological effect. They should be appropriate to the main theme of the lesson. The warm up should consist of activities which are vigorous and enjoyable. Accordingly, activities such as running, jumping, and rolling may be used. Emphasis should be on hard work. Following these activities children may be asked to practise a short sequence which they have previously developed. In addition to physiological and psychological considerations, teachers may also use the warm up as a time to develop a good atmosphere and establish firm control by use of direct commands.

The introduction of new core skill is best carried out as a class activity. This is a period of time when the whole class will often be practising the same activity albeit at different levels. It is imperative that the skill introduced is at a suitable level of difficulty for the majority of the children in the class. Once the children perceive that the skill is within their grasp they will have an attainable goal. This usually motivates the children to work enthusiastically at acquiring that skill. If it is too easy or too difficult then boredom will quickly set in and may cause discipline problems. After the introduction of a new skill, children will progress at varying rates, some finding it easy, others finding it difficult. Methods of dealing with this situation are discussed in the following sections concerned with learning stages.

Having decided which skill to introduce there are a number of considerations the teacher should make. Firstly, it is important that the complete picture is given to the pupils. They must have a clear idea of what is expected in terms of the movement to be produced. Gentile (1972) demonstrated the need to emphasise the objective of any skill. In order to communicate lucidly the nature of the movement, the teacher may use verbal explanation, visual, manual, and mechanical guidance in any combination and with differing degrees of emphasis.

> . . . 'in practice, the good instructor uses all the means of communication which are available to him. If one approach does not work he tries another.' (Lockhart 1966:66)

In any situation the environment provides more information than a person can attend to. Consequently he attends selectively to only part of the information available to him. When a teacher of gymnastics introduces a new core skill he should direct the attention of his pupils to the most relevant aspects. Thus if a teacher is using verbal explanation this should be kept to a minimum in the early stages and should be directed at the most important points for the acquisition of that skill. Excessive analysis and explanation of the movement during the introductory phase can cause 'information overload' leading to confusion and inability to select the correct basic movement response. In the backward roll for example, correct positioning of hands is essential for skilled performance. Learners should have their attention directed to this point before other aspects of the skill such as hip movement and the timing of the thrust are explained.

If the skill being taught is a relatively simple one verbal guidance may be sufficient. However, visual guidance, usually in the form of demonstration, appears to be more effective than verbalisation in the early stage of learning. A learner should be given a clear visual image of the required movement patterns. Since this mental image may fade it is usually necessary to provide a demonstration at frequent intervals. More often it is better to demonstrate at normal speed in order to show correct timing. A deliberately slow demonstration of a headspring to show how to overbalance in the angled position may only serve to teach poor timing of the hip action and leg throw. Principles relating to selective attention and information overload are applicable to visual guidance. Accordingly, in a complex skill the learner's attention should initially be directed to one or two aspects in order to prevent information overload and possible confusion. The introduction should present a clear picture of the whole skill thus a useful strategy may be to present a few successive demonstrations while the teacher draws the attention of his pupils to the important points of technique. When introducing the neckspring on the cross box, for example, a teacher may use the first demonstration to show the class the whole skill. During subsequent demonstrations he may direct the children's attention to the position of the shoulders on the box top, the position of the legs prior to the thrust, the hip action and the thrust from the arms respectively. Once the children are aware of these features they can see the relevance and relationships of the various part practices which follow.

In a later chapter theoretical aspects of skills acquisition are discussed from contrasting perspectives, for example, the behaviourist and the information processing approach. Both viewpoints emphasise the importance of providing a clear objective together with a good explanation and demonstration when the skill is introduced. Behaviourists refer to 'determining terminal behavioural responses', ie performing a backward roll to finish in straddle and the need to 'prime the behaviour segment or the behaviour itself'. This may involve for example, a clear demonstration and verbal explanation. Information processing theorists use the term 'concept of purpose' (Miller 1967). They suggest that the performer must develop arousal toward a specific goal or goals. A teacher should not make the assumption that his objectives are the same as the children's in a gymnastics lesson. A teacher's objective may be to help children gain new skills, the children's objectives may be to repeat old skills, avoid learning new ones because of the difficulties involved, or just to enjoy themselves or even misbehave. Fitts and Posner (1973:11–14) described three phases of learning, the early or cognitive phase, the intermediate or associative phase and the final or autonomous phase. They pointed out that during the early or cognitive stage of learning, instructions and demonstrations are most effective. A sound introduction therefore is extremely important for successful performance.

The time spent on explanation and demonstration during the introduction of a skill will vary according to the nature of the skill and the teacher's strategy. If the introduction is to be followed by a number of orientation activities designed to build up background experiences then a brief introduction may suffice. A teacher may, for example, briefly introduce the handspring to a group and then arrange for the children to practise a variety of orientation activities where they take their weight on their hands and pass through the handstand position. A more detailed introduction may then follow after the orientation activities. Conversely, a teacher may decide to omit orientation activities. In this case the introduction is immediately prior to the first part practice of the whole skill and the teacher may decide to spend considerably longer on his introduction, showing clearly the main features for successful performance.

2   Orientation activities

In more advanced movements the difficulties in developing sound technique are compounded by problems associated with body orientation as, for example, when the gymnast is airborne. The feelings of internal disorientation arising from somersaults and twists along with the effects of external forces often applied from unfamiliar directions can form a real barrier in understanding correct technique. It is by constant exposure to such sensations that the inhibiting effects are minimised.

The function of orientation activities is to simulate, in part, the feelings the gymnast would experience when performing a particular skill. When learning the flic-flac, for example, pupils may be asked to perform a variety of movements where they fall backwards, take their weight on their hands then bring their feet over to a standing position. Various pieces of apparatus may be used to simplify the move, eg, inclined box, safety mattress over a box top. Accordingly, the activities may be practised safely by children of relatively low gymnastic ability.

An orientation activity for the flic-flac

It may help to regard orientation activities as the first step in 'the progressive practices' sequence. Concern here should be more with the fun and enjoyment aspects rather than with technique training. These sessions can be useful to the teacher as they often develop motivation within children to acquire skills. Children, having played with a particular skill at this level, often demand to learn it 'properly'. It is important, however, that even at this level a gymnast has a clear idea of the end product and is then able to relate the feelings experienced during the practice of the skill itself.

Orientation activities may not always be necessary when learning a new skill and the teacher will decide whether to use them or not. His decisions will be based on factors relating to his specific situation. He will have to consider such factors as the spread of abilities within the class, the age of the pupils, their background experience, their motivation level and, not least, the amount and quality of the apparatus at his disposal. It is possible to devise many orientation activities but this will be of little use unless there is apparatus available to build suitable, safe situations.

At the outset of this section reference was made to complex skills. This is, of course, a relative term and a teacher may consider certain skills to be so simple as not to require orientation activities. Indeed, some basic core skills and their variations will themselves become orientation activities for subsequent more complex activities, for example, rolling activities may serve as orientation activities for somersaults.

3 Class activity work on a core skill

During this stage children should be taught to perform the core skill with good technique. Methods used by teachers will vary according to the skills, the ability of the performers and the apparatus available (this latter aspect is discussed towards the end of the chapter in the section on introducing skills to specific groups within a class). The comments included here assume that *class activity* work on a particular skill is possible. The importance of selecting a skill at an appropriate level for the class has already been discussed. It is equally important that the teacher carries out a careful analysis of the nature of the skill that he is to introduce. The complexity of the movement will determine whether or not progressive practices will assist the pupils to acquire the skill.

In the early lessons which arise from a scheme of work on traditional gymnastics the core skills such as rolls and cartwheels will be relatively simple. It is unnecessary therefore for a teacher to break down a movement into component parts to develop good technique. The cartwheel, for example, should be attempted as a whole with the initial emphasis concerned with lifting the legs as high as possible. Since it is a novel skill, the class will normally find initial practice of the whole movement enjoyable and stimulating. This is because progress usually follows a normal curve of learning, ie during initial trials there are rapid increases in performance. This period of learning can be most rewarding and exciting for the children. However, since children possess differing degrees of abilities, the rate of progress will vary considerably one

individual to another. It then becomes imperative that teachers adapt their approach to suit both slow and quick learners. This may sound a difficult situation but in reality usually only involves the teacher in varying his approach for relatively few of the class. Different levels of ability produce a wide range of performance levels but a teacher will be primarily involved in helping the majority of the class to acquire better technique and style on the core skill. Depending on ability he may need to suggest to a few children either a simpler or more difficult variation based on a core skill. With the cartwheel, for example, one boy who is having difficulty may be asked to perform a half cartwheel and lower to front support. Another pupil, who quickly performs a technically sound cartwheel may be asked to produce two consecutive cartwheels or a one handed cartwheel. Strictly speaking these are variations and a separate section on these movements is included later in this chapter. Eventually the whole class will be taught variations on many core skills, however, the teacher's approach should be flexible. If it is appropriate to introduce a variation to one or two boys during this stage of teaching then a teacher should do so.

The emphasis in this stage of presentation is on developing correct technique and in order to do this it may be necessary to break down the skill and teach progressive practices. This method of teaching is also advocated if during the early learning stages there is a danger of injury to the pupil. Care must be taken in deciding on how to break down the skill. The relevance of the parts must be clearly seen by the pupil and the acquisition of each part should make a positive contribution to the acquisition of the whole skill.

Although the ultimate aim is to help each child acquire the whole skill a teacher should regard each part as a separate skill. Accordingly, each segment will require an introduction, explanation and demonstration. A progressive practices approach to teaching skills can help a teacher cope with the problem of mixed ability. The more able will quickly acquire the parts and soon learn the whole skill. The less able will take longer but if a teacher emphasises that each part should be regarded as a separate skill then every boy may find his practice both challenging and rewarding.

The teaching of a core skill through progressive practices may be illustrated by outlining an approach to teaching the neckspring vault. The apparatus should be arranged as shown in the diagram below. Initially the children will be asked to run, take off two feet and roll along the platform.

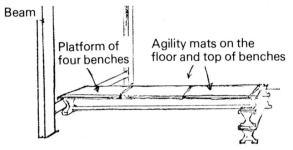

Beam

Platform of four benches

Agility mats on the floor and top of benches

Platform for neckspring progressions

The following progressions will then be introduced to individuals when they have acquired each preceding part.
(i)   Roll, keeping legs straight, trying to stop with weight on hands and shoulders, and knees over nose.
(ii) Stand on the platform, crouch down, roll to the edge then throw the feet away raising the hips and pushing off the hands.

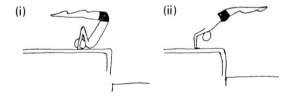

(i)   (ii)

(iii) Place a box in front of the platform. The box should be at the same height as the platform of benches. Those who have acquired the early parts may now try to roll so that the head is tucked under and the body weight goes onto the box top with the shoulders in contact with the box. The move is continued so that the boy rolls onto the platform.

(iii)

(iv) Once this skill has been achieved the learner should attempt to join the parts. The box should be placed out on its own and surrounded by mats. The learner approaches, takes off two feet, rolls onto his shoulders and throws the feet away to finish standing. It is advisable for the teacher to give support to the initial attempts since fear may disrupt the co-ordination of the parts. However, after a few successful trials this fear usually disappears.
(v)   Finally, a full-size box with springboard and mats may be arranged. The skill acquired on the low box usually transfers readily to a higher box.

The identification of all the parts in sequential order, that must be practised if the complete skill is to be performed, is an aspect of sound teaching. How these parts exist in relation to each other at different levels of skills acquisition has interested sports psychologists. Some have taken the standpoint that man, like a computer, functions with *higher order (executive) routines* and *subroutines*. The executive programme of a straddle vault on the long horse, for example, incorporates many subroutines. These include a co-ordinated running action, a jump onto two feet on the springboard, a full stretch to place the hands on the far end of the horse, a push off the box with the feet being brought round and finally a controlled bending into a crouched position on landing.

When attention must be paid to a specific part or subroutine in order to produce the complete skill then that part may be considered to be a higher order subroutine. Parts which are performed accurately without conscious attention may be considered as lower order subroutines. During the learning of skills it appears that some higher order subroutines are delegated to lower order subroutines. Thus as a particular part becomes well learned it leaves the higher cortical system in the brain free to attend to other matters. A boy learning the neckspring by practising the various stages outlined above, for example, must initially concentrate on a roll onto the platform. Since this is his first attempt he has little choice but to attend to the basic feature of a controlled roll. Once this skill has been mastered he can progress to the next part practice of throwing the legs and raising the hips. Since attaining the correct position has been delegated to a lower order subroutine he can now attend to other aspects of the skill.

The subroutines may be considered as foundational building blocks, mastery at each level helping to acquire the complete skill. They may also be viewed in sequential format with each one contributing to the overall quality of the movement. Often the teacher's aim is to help a child acquire a subroutine and delegate it to a lower order where it can operate without conscious attention being given to it. Accordingly, teachers should not be continually asking children to think about what his arms or legs are doing. Attention should be directed to the specific subroutine which needs to be acquired or improved technically. Thus a child performing the straddle vault on the long horse should only be asked to think about the height of his legs when he can place his hands on the far end without having to think about it. One of the skills of teaching and coaching is being aware of when a child is ready to progress to a new part practice. In addition, teachers must be able to observe childrens' performances and select the major fault. This should be corrected before attention is given to more minor faults.

The theoretical principles relating to progressive practices are discussed more fully in a later chapter. The need to break down complex skills is recognised by both *behaviourists* and *information processing* theorists. The former refer to the need to determine the appropriate sequence for teaching segments and their amalgamation so that the skill may be built efficiently. The latter refer to great uncertainty and high information load which can overload a person's information processing system when the beginner attempts a complex skill as a whole. He is unable to attend to and process all the information at once.

In general, if whole practice is possible then it should be done as it usually results in more rapid learning. However, if the skill is complex, or if the learner is less able, or there is any degree of danger, then progressive practices may be advisable.

During this learning stage the teacher is helping the children acquire a specific movement pattern. Whether the children are attempting a core skill as a whole or working on a practice a teacher should aim to condition a response which is technically correct. In order to do this, each successful performance should be reinforced with praise and encouragement. Hopefully, this will encourage the learner to repeat the movement pattern. The use of praise should be considered carefully. If praise is given when

the movement is not technically sound then there is a likelihood of that movement pattern being repeated. If a boy is working hard by all means praise his effort, progress, or the aspects of his performance which are good, but avoid giving praise when it is unjustified. If poor movements are positively reinforced by praise from a teacher there is a likelihood that those movements will be repeated.

Of all the factors influencing skills acquisition it has been argued that feedback is the most important aspect. Feedback refers to the information the individual gains from his performance which permits him to profit from the experience. This information arrives both throughout and on completion of a movement when the performer becomes aware of the results of his action. It may also arrive as new information from external sources such as the teacher, coach or videotape. Thus the experienced gymnast who kicks up too slowly for a handspring will be receiving feedback from his proprioceptors, (ie sense receptors in the muscles, tendons and joints) which will inform him that his flight is too slow. He will soon be painfully aware of the results of this unless he quickly adjusts his body position. The effect of feedback is to cause future responses to be regulated. Accordingly, the gymnast may try to swing up much more quickly for his next attempt.

Feedback information from the teacher or coach is important for the acquisition of gymnastic skills. The gymnast is usually unable to see many of his body parts during a particular movement, consequently he needs to be given information on the quality of the move from external sources. It is most important that the teacher has the observational and analytical skills to enable him to give the child accurate knowledge of performance and indicate how improvement may be attained. It is also advisable that a teacher has an understanding of the concepts related to feedback such as providing optimal level of information, the effects of its delay and its motivational function. In recent years the value of videotape as a source of knowledge of performance has been receiving increasing attention. (Selder, D.J., Del Rolan, N. 1979.) The findings have important implications for coaching.

If a teacher is taking a class of 20 or 30 children he should bear in mind that many of them will be producing movements which he cannot see. If a boy is successfully regaining his feet after, for example, a forward roll straddle but has very bent knees he may tend to repeat that pattern of movement as it has brought success thus providing positive reinforcement. A teacher should observe his class carefully, therefore, and provide knowledge of performance to improve the quality of the skill. In the example above, landing on the feet brings a feeling of success but this only serves to consolidate poor technique.

Reference has been made to the value of orientation activities as promoting fun and enjoyment and to the necessity of selecting skills which are appropriate to the level of ability of the children. These are important considerations which influence children's motivation to acquire gymnastic skills. There is evidence to suggest that humans have an innate drive for competence, that is, a desire for effective functioning (White 1959). Other needs, for example, activity and achievement result in children being 'skills hungry'. The manner in which this intrinsic motivation is managed by teachers greatly influences children's attitudes to gymnastics. Helping children to satisfy their needs by successfully acquiring skills may further develop their interest and motivation. In order to do this a teacher must be able to help children develop realistic goals and aspirations and ensure good performance is rewarded. In traditional gymnastics teachers should set performance to these standards. They will be clearly aware when they have been successful. Accordingly, lessons should be planned carefully to ensure that every child experiences some degree of success.

An understanding of motivation and related concepts such as needs, drives, expectancy, arousal are important for sound teaching. A separate chapter has been devoted to motivation since in recent years considerable advancement in coaching technique have resulted from investigations into motivation. (Rushall, B. 1979, Straub, W.F. 1978, Landers, D. 1980.)

4 Skill expansion activities

Once a core skill has been acquired, the teacher's next task is to create situations where the skill is developed in a more challenging environment. Cartwheels, for example, may be performed along bench tops. The essential purposes of skill expansion activities are therefore twofold, firstly to develop the core skill and

secondly to maintain the relationship with the initial activity. Thus such factors as technique, style and co-ordination which were stressed at the outset are still emphasised. The simple forward roll, for example, may be made more challenging by asking the children to perform the move along box tops and benches, around bars or after diving over an obstacle.

In vaulting, skill expansion activities may simply involve increasing the amplitude of the move in order to make it more challenging. The difference between the 'leap frog' and the straddle vault performed from a spring board over a long horse, for example, is mainly a difference in amplitude. By arranging apparatus so that an increase in speed and effort is required in order to perform the vault successfully, the teacher can provide challenging situations appropriate to a wide range of ability.

In addition to varying the amplitude of a vault it may be made more challenging by asking the children to vary their point of contact with the box. A through vault on the long box, for example, may be performed either after landing in crouch on the front end, or after placing the hands directly on the far end or after placing the hands on the front end.

5 Variations

When children have become proficient at a core skill it is possible to introduce selected variations. During this stage of learning the whole class should be made aware of the wide variety of options, eg, jump into place with half turn, tuck jump, straddle jump, full turn, half turn direct into forward roll, etc. It should be remembered that a few children may have already practised variations during the teaching of a core skill, consequently these children can be used to demonstrate the skills they have acquired. This is often better than the teacher demonstrating because of perceptual difficulties related to the size difference between pupil and teacher. Variations usually involve either a change in the starting or finishing position or both. Good examples in variations in starting and finishing positions are illustrated under the *Ins and Outs of Rolls* in Chapter Two. By starting at one of the positions shown on the left hand side and going through to one of the positions shown on the right hand side a variation on the forward roll is produced. Moving from the right to the left produces a variation on the backward roll. Only a few starting and finishing positions are shown. There are many more but the illustration is not intended to be comprehensive but merely to indicate an approach which is simple to understand and easy to develop. In addition to introducing specific variations, teachers may also allow time for children to develop their own variations based on a particular core skill.

Once a teacher has a wide knowledge of variations based on the core skill he is able to give direct teaching to the whole class. The teaching approach may be formal and will be appropriate to a wide range of ability. Children may, for example, be working on the handstand. The sequence would be therefore, firstly the introduction of the skill, secondly orientation activities, thirdly class activity, fourthly skill expansion activities and fifthly the introduction of variations. During this latter stage the less able may be encouraged to practise easier balances, eg, where the weight is taken on the hands with knees on elbows. The more able may move sideways into handstand or learn to curl up off two feet into handstand. All the children will be working on balancing on the hands and the teacher's role is to give direct teaching aimed at helping them gain specific skills at their own level of ability. Every child should be asked to work on a particular variation which is challenging. This hopefully will lead to pleasure and satisfaction once the skill is acquired. Since the specific response is necessary the criteria for good quality can readily be identified. Throughout his teaching it is imperative that a teacher emphasises good quality and control.

Variations based on core skills are more easily developed for floor exercises than for vaults. There are obviously relatively few variations of the neckspring compared to the forward roll. In fact, a variation is usually considered a different vault. However the teacher is still faced with the same problems arising from mixed ability. A possible answer may be to arrange his apparatus in varying degrees of difficulty with the children working on apparatus most suited to their level of ability. Children may, for example, be introduced to the through vault by using boxes, beams with saddles attached and pommelled horses. The more able should use the boxes and the less able the apparatus on which it is easier to perform the through vault. A similar organisation may be used when teaching variations on a core skill which has been acquired by the majority of the class. For example, if the basic bent leg through vault has been acquired by the majority, the teacher may decide it is appropriate to introduce to the class variations such as straight leg through vault or through vault half turn. In this case the more able pupils learning the more difficult vault may benefit by reverting to the use of beam saddles.

The use of variations is necessary from a motivational aspect. Children are 'skills hungry' and this need can best be satisfied if children are given goals which are seen to be both attainable and challenging. If a teacher demonstrates expectations that are either too low or too high the motivation so essential for good peformance and skills learning will rapidly disappear.

6 Sequence development

The sequence is the culmination, the high point for which the gymnast has been aiming while practising his gymnastic skills. It involves the selection and combination and a number of skills linked together to form a sequence. A sequence created and composed by the gymnast, containing his skill variations and combinations and performed thoughtfully, can bear the stamp of his own individuality and personality. However, even at this level when the gymnast has learned basic skills and created personal variations it is usually still necessary for the teacher to indicate the ways in which combinations can be made and/or improved. He should explain that the sequence can be made more interesting and satisfying by displaying a variety of movements. The routine can take on a different character by taking into consideration variations such as different starting and finishing positions, shape, speed, direction and levels of working.

Dive forward roll to one leg (dynamic start and variation of forward roll); round off (variation on cartwheel); jump with three quarter turn (variation on straight jump giving change of direction and focus). (diagram A)

Step forward and arabesque (balance, change of pace); kick to handstand and roll down to sit (variation on forward roll); backward roll to front support (variation on backward roll). (diagram B)

Pull forward to roll (variation on forward roll); jump with full turn (variation on straight jump). (diagram C)

As individual competence, vocabulary of skills and variations increase so can the sequence produced becomes more complex and interesting. Whilst the sequences are composed

by individual pupils, according to their own levels of attainment, the teacher should be vigilant on two main counts. Firstly, that individual pupils are not working 'within themselves' but are continually encouraged to make full use of their abilities. Secondly, that quality is not forfeited for the benefit of complexity or difficulty. When a number of core skills have been introduced sequences should be composed of a range of skills and variations. At this stage teachers should ensure that individual sequences are not dominated by one particular skill. One good reason for teaching the whole class a single sequence, initially, is to reinforce the importance of quality of performance.

The practice of such a sequence may be made more interesting for the more able by forming small groups of two, three or four, which then perform the sequence in unison, cannon, opposition. Great enjoyment and working co-operation can be achieved in this fashion. Another teaching strategy is to divide the class into small groups and give each group a work card on which is illustrated a simple sequence. Each group then performs its sequence after being allowed suitable time period for practice. The

other groups are then encouraged to constructively criticise the performances. An experienced teacher will be able to think of other motivational methods.

A strategy for introducing skills to specific groups

Teaching methods based on utilising some or all of the six stages outlined above should allow teachers to introduce and develop a wide range of core skills along with their variations. However, once the children have been introduced to a large number of core skills, differences in ability may become an increasing problem. It is soon obvious that some pupils are ready to be introduced to more advanced skills. The introduction of variations based on a core skill caters for this problem but only to a certain extent. In order to ensure that the children are working at as high a level as possible, the teacher may consider introducing a new more advanced skill to a specific group. This can be arranged by planning a lesson so that the children work in groups throughout. The groups should be organised so that the pupils capable of more advanced skills are in the same group or groups. At the start of the lesson a variety of apparatus should be arranged for the practice of previously taught skills. Groups should rotate around practising on each piece of apparatus during the lesson. Thus the teacher is able to work with a particular group introducing a new skill. He may, for example, decide to introduce the front somersault on the mat. Once the warm up has been carried out and the apparatus arranged, he can position himself at the mat to work initially with a particular group. It is most important, however, that he does not devote any more of his time to the more able pupils than to the less able pupils. A useful strategy is for the teacher to remain teaching at the mat for the majority of the lesson. As the groups rotate from one piece of apparatus to another he will be able to give individual guidance and encouragement to every boy in the class. Just as the more able are introduced to a new advanced skill so the teacher should introduce a new skill at the appropriate level of difficulty to other groups. Clearly it is important that those pupils who are not involved with the teacher are practising previously acquired skills. It may be that to achieve this objective physical support is required. The authors are cognisant of this fact and a detailed section related to all forms of support and its organisation is included in Chapter Two.

The strategy outlined above may also be used when a teacher wishes to introduce a core skill to the whole class but is unable to do so through lack of apparatus. It may be decided for example, to introduce the upward circle on the beam. The teacher should base his lesson on group practice throughout but position himself at the beam. The groups will rotate around each piece of apparatus and when they arrive at the beam will be taught the upward circle. In order to save unnecessary repetition the teacher should introduce the skill to the whole class at the start of the lesson and then repeat instructions and demonstrations when necessary to specific groups or individuals.

Teaching method for introducing a skill in a group work lesson should follow the basic principles outlined for teaching core skills. However, it is unlikely that all six stages will be employed. Since the rest of the class will be using much of the apparatus available it is unlikely that orientation activities and skill expansion activities could be used for a particular group. Accordingly, the teacher should concentrate on

a good introduction and appropriate practices.

Summary

The approach to teaching gymnastics outlined in this chapter is based on the assumption that the teacher is setting out with the aim of helping children to develop specific gymnastic skills. In order to achieve this aim a direct teaching method should be used. However, unlike the rigid direct method used some years ago we are suggesting a more flexible approach to allow for a wide range of ability. This approach is possible if the teacher possesses an in depth knowledge of 'core skills' and the numerous variations based on each of these skills. The core skills selected should be appropriate to the range of abilities within the class, the children's background experience and the apparatus available. It is not sufficient simply to introduce and help develop a range of core skills on their own. Various stages should be used whenever possible.

1   INTRODUCING SKILLS

The lesson should start with an active warm up designed to prepare the children both psychologically and physiologically. The skill which the teacher aims to develop should be clearly introduced. A visual demonstration is often important in order that children are made aware of the relevance of the various practices which follow. If the core skill being taught is relatively simple, the children may commence to practise their skills immediately after an introduction. However, if they are complex it may be advisable to teach a number of orientation activities prior to allowing practice of the skills itself.

2   ORIENTATION ACTIVITIES

The function of orientation activities is to simulate in part the feelings that the gymnast would experience when performing a particular skill. Through these activities children can develop confidence in, for example, falling backwards onto the hands. Hopefully, this will reduce the high anxiety which children may otherwise experience during their first attempts at difficult skills. During the teaching of orientation activities, the emphasis should be on enjoyment.

3   CLASS ACTIVITY ON CORE SKILLS

The teacher should be able to apply the basic concepts related to skills acquisition. He must, for example, decide whether to use a whole or a part-whole method. If the latter is used, the progressive practices should be designed to ensure that positive transfer occurs. Knowledge of principles related to aspects of skills acquisition, such as guidance, reinforcement, feedback and motivation are essential for good teaching. The core skill should be taught as a class activity with the children initially practising the same skill or progression. However, after a few attempts it may be necessary for some children to practise easier or harder variations.

4   SKILL EXPANSION ACTIVITIES

When children have become proficient in the performance of a core skill, the teacher's next task is to create situations where the skill is developed in a more challenging environment.

5   VARIATIONS

If an individual skill has been mastered by the majority of the class, it then becomes possible to teach selected variations. A number of skills may be introduced to the class in order to make the children aware of the wide variety of options. They can then select skills appropriate to their level of ability. Many variations can be achieved by varying the starting and finishing positions of core skills or modifying the apparatus for vaults.

6   SEQUENCE DEVELOPMENT

This involves the selection and combination of skills linked together to form a floor exercise. Children may include the core skills which they have acquired together with their favourite variations. Once a number of specific skills have been acquired, children may create their own modifications and linking moves to develop a good sequence.

Introducing skills to specific groups

Once the children have acquired a number of core skills, it may be appropriate to arrange ability groups. Using this organisation a teacher can introduce new skills at an appropriate level of difficulty to each group. He should position himself at one piece of apparatus throughout most of the lesson with the groups moving around to work on each piece of apparatus. Thus each child receives individual guidance. This organisation may also be used in order to introduce skills which cannot be taught as a class activity because of insufficient apparatus.

CHAPTER TWO

The core skills

In this chapter a number of skills will be examined under the headings proposed in Chapter One. For each skill a series of orientation activities will be introduced. This will be followed by details of good technique, supporting methods, skill expansion activities, variations and finally, ideas for incorporating the skill into a sequence.

In an attempt to further explain our approach the following diagram has been drawn using the core skill of the forward roll as an example. It shows how a large number of gymnastic skills can be created and developed by using a combination of skill expansion activities and skill variations. Teachers should note that sequence construction phases may be introduced at any point after Stage 2 has been reached.

The forward roll

Stage 1	Stage 2	Stage 3	Stage 4	Stage 5
Orientation activities	The technique of the core skill	Skill expansion activities	Skill variations	Skill expansion activities based on the variations

FORWARD ROLL

Stage 3:
on mats
on benches
on box tops
over obstacles
over partners
down inclines
between ropes
. . . etc

Stage 4:
roll to sit
roll to knees ($\frac{1}{4}$ turn)
roll to back lying
roll to one leg
roll to straddle sit
roll to shoulder stand
roll with straight legs
roll to 'V' balance
. . . etc

Stage 5:
Each of the variations may now be practised in a variety of situations, eg, over boxes, along benches, on mats . . . etc

The variety of skills with their relative difficulties, coupled with the many possible apparatus situations, allows each child to work on activities suitable to his/her individual ability level

Possibility of sequence development

Possibility of sequence development

Forward and backward rolls

ORIENTATION ACTIVITIES

THE TECHNIQUE

Following the practice of the orientation
exercises, where the emphasis is on challenge
and enjoyment, the teacher should aim to
develop good technique at an early stage before
pupils acquire poor quality movement.

Basic practice: rocking backward and forward
taking the weight on hands then heels . . .

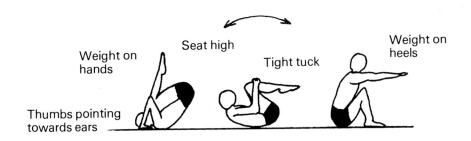

Weight on
hands

Seat high

Tight tuck

Weight on
heels

Thumbs pointing
towards ears

Forward roll

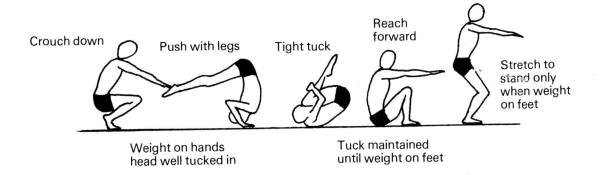

Crouch down

Push with legs

Tight tuck

Reach
forward

Stretch to
stand only
when weight
on feet

Weight on hands
head well tucked in

Tuck maintained
until weight on feet

Backward roll

Crouch down

Tight tuck
chest on knees

Push hard
keep tuck

Hands in
position early

Keep pushing to
land on balls of feet

SKILL EXPANSION ACTIVITIES

Once good technique has been established the
skill should be expanded by introducing more
challenging but similar movements. Some such
situations are illustrated below:

VARIATIONS

As stated earlier in the book it is possible to produce many variations on the basic element by starting and finishing in different positions or/and by changing the shape of the body whilst performing the skill. The diagram below illustrates a few such starting and finishing positions. Clearly many more are possible and, we contend, that it is at this stage that the child should be encouraged to explore the possibilities for himself with only guidance from the teacher.

THE 'INS AND OUTS' OF THE ROLL

SEQUENCES

Sequence 1

Short run, stretched jump (basic jump), forward roll to sit with straight legs (roll variation), half backward roll to shoulder stand (basic balance), tucked forward roll into high jump, land correctly.

Sequence 2

Forward roll to straddle stand (variation on forward roll), reach between legs and tucked forward roll to stand (basic roll).

Sequence 3

Crouch down and high straddled stretched jump (variation on stretched jump), tucked forward roll (basic skill), high jump with half turn (variation on basic jump), tucked backward roll (basic skill).

The headstand

ORIENTATION ACTIVITIES

 Beam or
bar

THE TECHNIQUE

Legs straight.
Walk in on tip toes

Head and hands form
triangular pattern
on floor

Press down hard with hands

Keep nose
just touching
floor

When feet come clear of the floor lift legs into

. . . bent legged . . .
headstand

or . . . straight legged
headstand.

Back kept
firmly straight

THE SUPPORT

Supporter close to gymnast

Hands hold hips

Kneeling down with knees shoulder width apart

SKILL EXPANSION ACTIVITIES

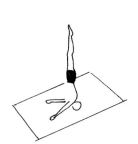

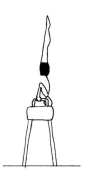

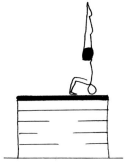

VARIATIONS:
THE 'INS AND OUTS' OF THE HEADSTAND

SEQUENCES

The cartwheel

ORIENTATION ACTIVITIES

THE SUPPORT

Hands hold hips

First hand in position early

Follow through support
until skill completed

THE TECHNIQUE

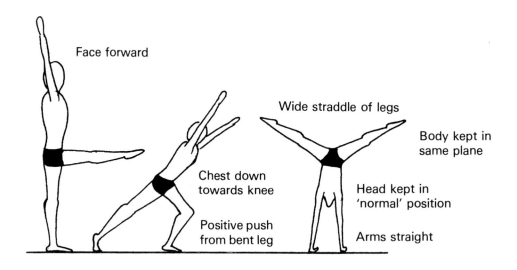

Face forward

Wide straddle of legs

Body kept in same plane

Chest down towards knee

Head kept in 'normal' position

Positive push from bent leg

Arms straight

No hollowing of the back

Eyes looking at hand on floor

Foot brought close to hand

THE HAND AND FOOT PATTERN

Straight line through each point of contact

SKILL EXPANSION ACTIVITIES

VARIATIONS:
THE 'INS AND OUTS' OF THE CARTWHEEL

SEQUENCES

The handstand

ORIENTATION ACTIVITIES

Most of these activities may be used as a 'play way' approach to help develop the necessary strength in the shoulder girdle.

THE TECHNIQUE AND SUPPORT

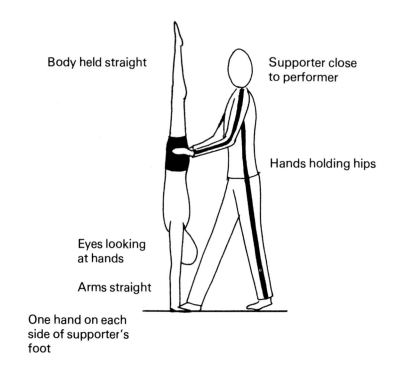

Body held straight

Supporter close
to performer

Hands holding hips

Eyes looking
at hands

Arms straight

One hand on each
side of supporter's
foot

SKILL EXPANSION ACTIVITIES

The handstand is a relatively advanced skill
when considered as a balance. The balances illustrated below will take much practice and consequently support is advised.

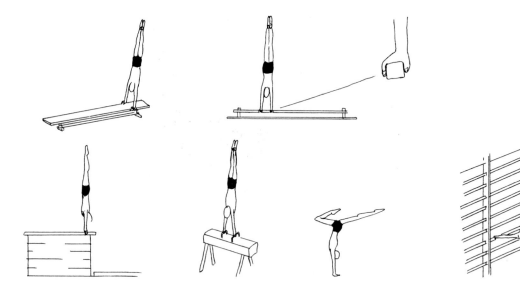

VARIATIONS: THE 'INS AND OUTS' OF THE HANDSTAND

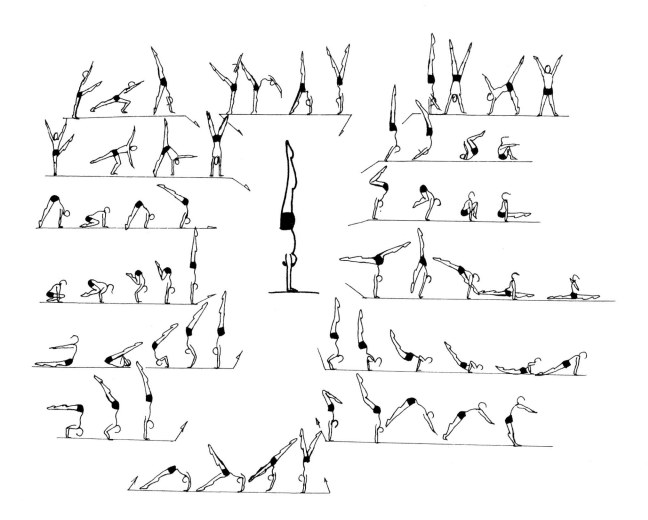

The headspring and neckspring

These two moves are so similar in essence that they are considered together. With very few obvious exceptions the practices, skill expansion activities and variations are suitable for either skill. The neckspring, however, is relatively much more difficult than the headspring requiring greater strength and dynamism owing to the lower starting point of the centre of gravity.

ORIENTATION ACTIVITIES

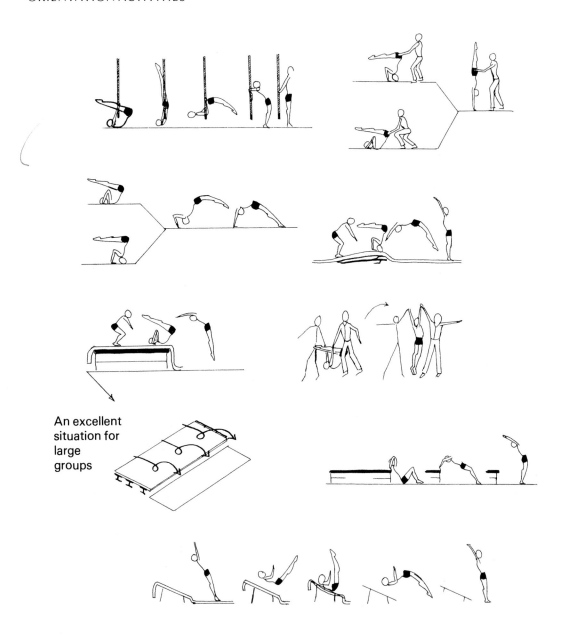

An excellent situation for large groups

THE TECHNIQUE

Hips lead body off balance

Hands almost in line with head

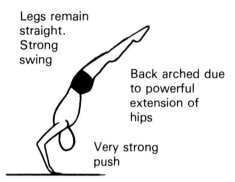

Legs remain straight. Strong swing

Back arched due to powerful extension of hips

Very strong push

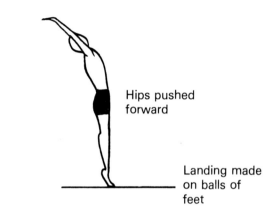

Hips pushed forward

Landing made on balls of feet

THE SUPPORT

Left hand in middle of back

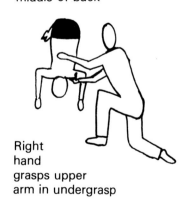

Right hand grasps upper arm in undergrasp

Elbows kept as close as possible to body

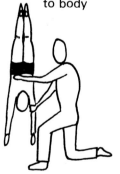

Press firmly on left foot to help lift gymnast

Right hand maintains grip until gymnast stands firm

Right hand ensures correct body shape

With taller gymnasts follow support through to stand

SKILL EXPANSION ACTIVITIES

VARIATIONS: THE 'INS AND OUTS' OF THE HEADSPRING/NECKSPRING

SEQUENCES

The through vault

This activity is taken as a core skill and treated the same way as the other core skills in this book. In the minds of most people the activity of vaulting is performed over a horse or box after jumping from a take-off board. In our approach, however, this form of the activity is only one point in the overview of the skill. The correct use of the vaulting board is covered elsewhere in this chapter.

ORIENTATION ACTIVITIES

The important coaching point which should be stressed throughout these initial practices is that the thrust from the apparatus is made using straight arms. It is not a bent arm to straight arm push but rather a dynamic extension of the shoulders.

THE TECHNIQUE

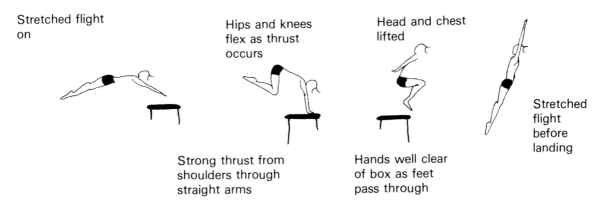

Stretched flight on

Hips and knees flex as thrust occurs

Head and chest lifted

Stretched flight before landing

Strong thrust from shoulders through straight arms

Hands well clear of box as feet pass through

THE SUPPORT (Supporter standing on left of performer)

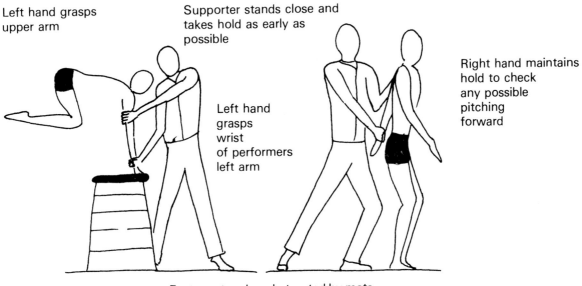

Left hand grasps upper arm

Supporter stands close and takes hold as early as possible

Left hand grasps wrist of performers left arm

Right hand maintains hold to check any possible pitching forward

Feet apart and unobstructed by mats

The partner activity illustrated is very suitable for teaching the supporting technique, and giving practice in it, to the children. The teacher should first fully explain the technique and demonstrate it. The pupils then work in groups of four with the teacher helping where required. As the pupils' confidence and competence increases the support can readily be transferred to other through vault situations.

SKILL EXPANSION ACTIVITIES

VARIATIONS

With the exceptions of the through vault with half turn (full turn ?) and the through vault with straight legs, this core skill does not lend itself to a large number of possible variations from the basic. The two variations mentioned above are illustrated. The advantage of this particular core skill is that of its potential use in many different apparatus situations. It is also possible to perform the skill throughout an enormous range of competence levels.

SEQUENCES

1.

2.

The handspring

ORIENTATION ACTIVITIES

THE SUPPORT

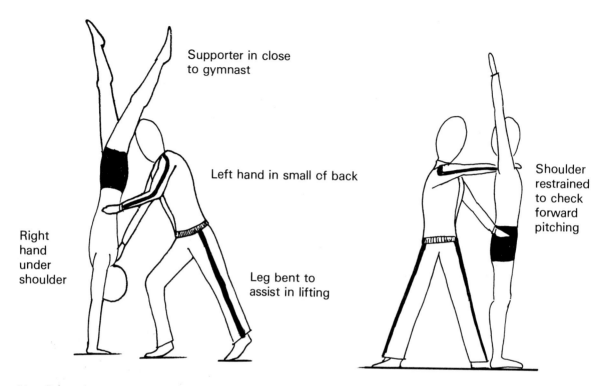

Supporter in close to gymnast

Left hand in small of back

Right hand under shoulder

Leg bent to assist in lifting

Shoulder restrained to check forward pitching

Note: the above comments are for a supporter standing on the left of the performer.

THE TECHNIQUE

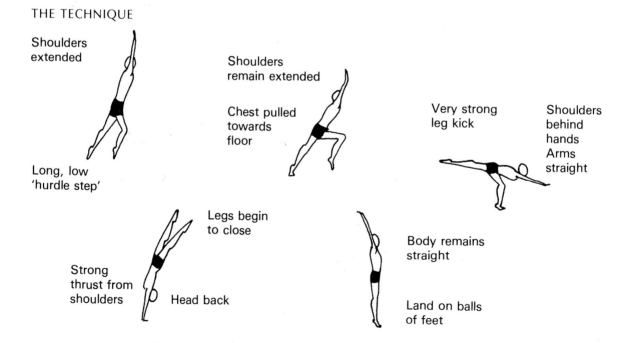

Shoulders extended

Long, low 'hurdle step'

Shoulders remain extended

Chest pulled towards floor

Very strong leg kick

Shoulders behind hands Arms straight

Strong thrust from shoulders

Legs begin to close

Head back

Body remains straight

Land on balls of feet

SKILL EXPANSION ACTIVITIES

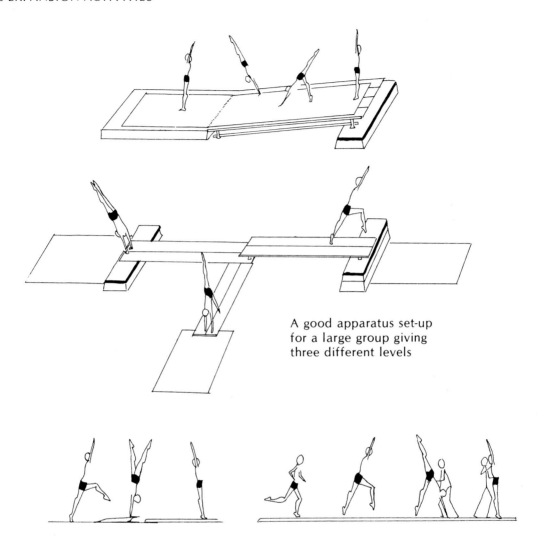

A good apparatus set-up
for a large group giving
three different levels

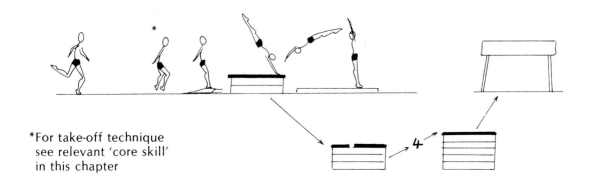

*For take-off technique
see relevant 'core skill'
in this chapter

VARIATIONS: THE 'INS AND OUTS' OF THE HANDSPRING

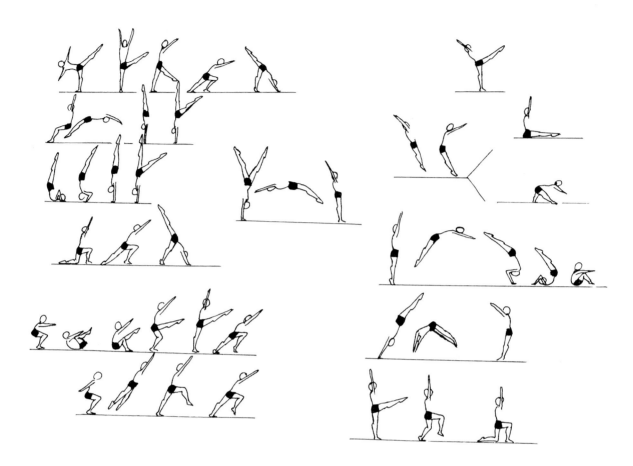

SEQUENCES

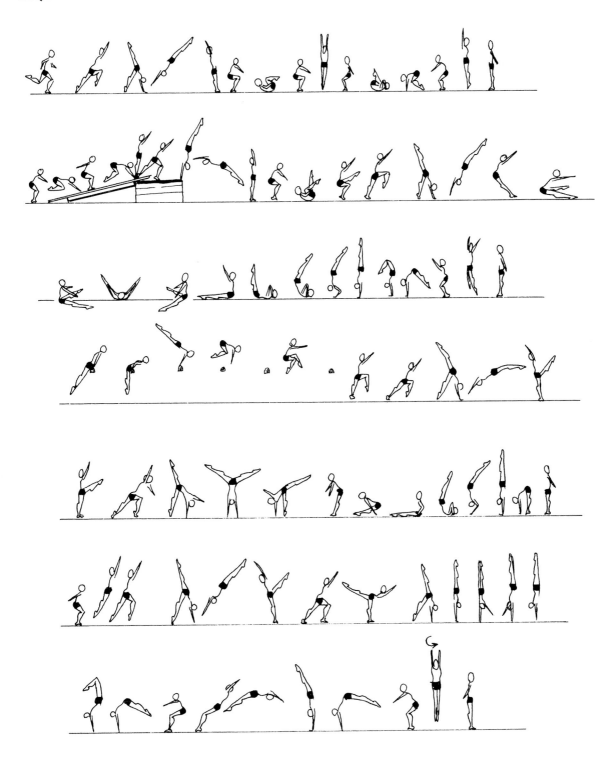

The flic-flac

ORIENTATION ACTIVITIES

Adequate matting is required
as performer may roll sideways
in initial stages

The height of the support
is critical. Too high and
the performer will not turn
over. Too low and the supporters
will be unable to lift the
performer safely

THE TECHNIQUE

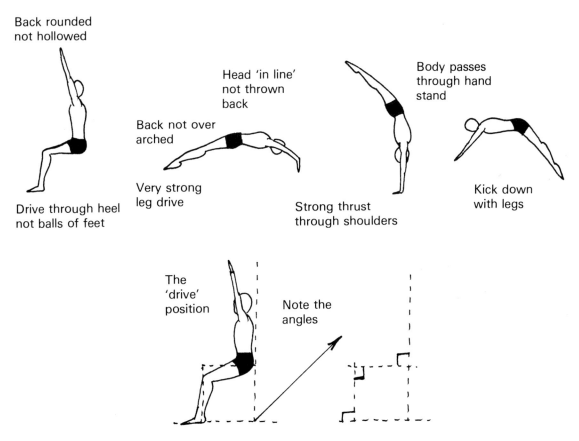

Back rounded
not hollowed

Head 'in line'
not thrown
back

Body passes
through hand
stand

Back not over
arched

Drive through heel
not balls of feet

Very strong
leg drive

Strong thrust
through shoulders

Kick down
with legs

The
'drive'
position

Note the
angles

THE SUPPORT

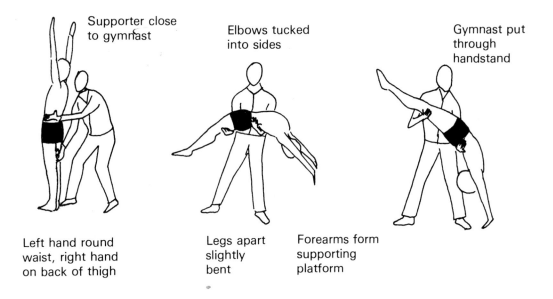

Supporter close
to gymnast

Elbows tucked
into sides

Gymnast put
through
handstand

Left hand round
waist, right hand
on back of thigh

Legs apart
slightly
bent

Forearms form
supporting
platform

SKILL EXPANSION ACTIVITIES

It will be necessary to support the gymnast through each of these activities until confidence and competence increases sufficiently for the performer to accomplish the skill safely.

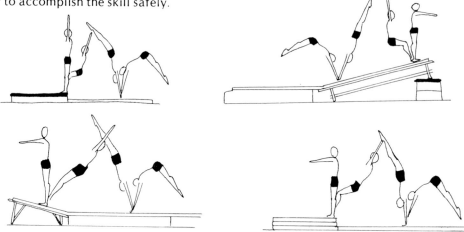

VARIATIONS: THE 'INS AND OUTS' OF THE FLIC-FLAC

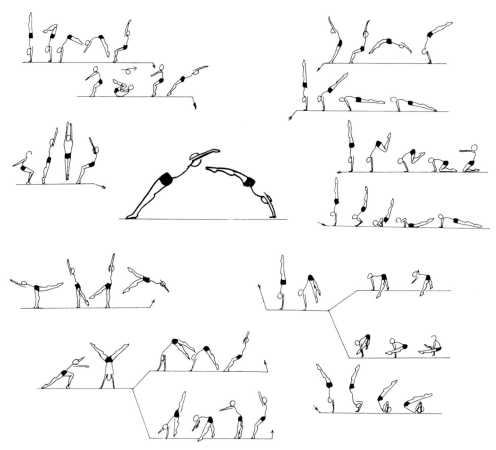

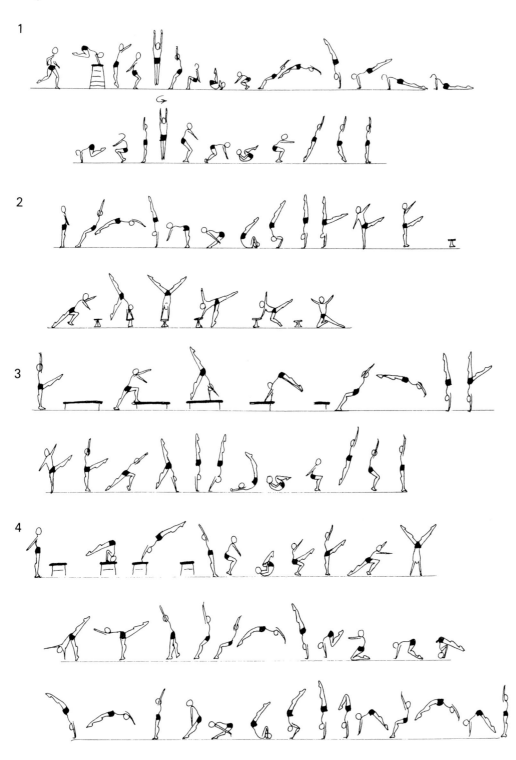

SEQUENCES

1

2

3

4

The underswing dismount

This skill may be performed from either a conventional beam or a bar.

ORIENTATION ACTIVITIES

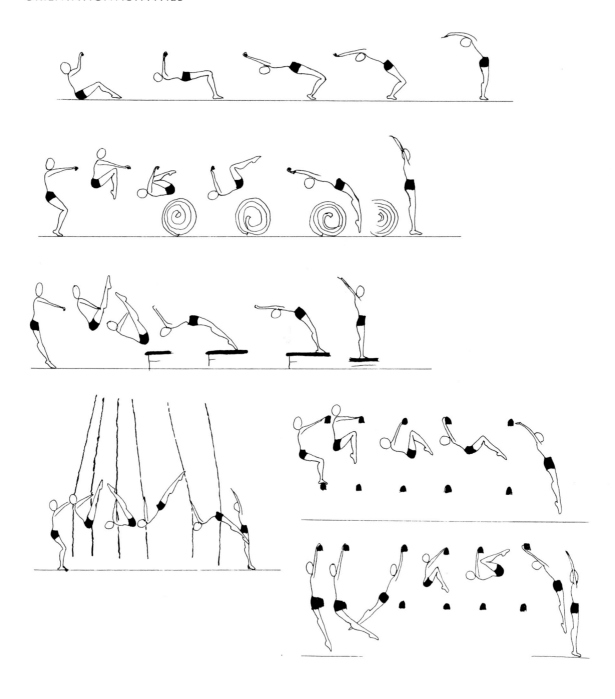

THE TECHNIQUE

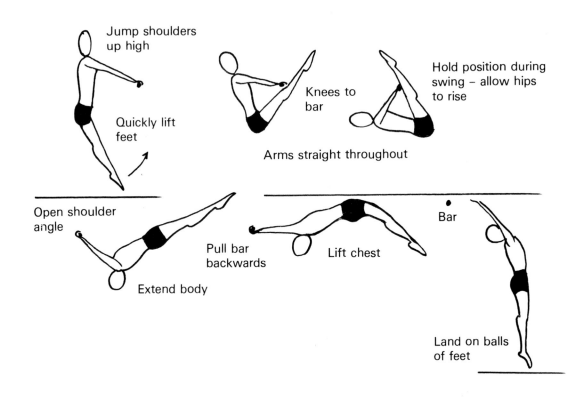

Jump shoulders up high

Quickly lift feet

Knees to bar

Hold position during swing – allow hips to rise

Arms straight throughout

Open shoulder angle

Pull bar backwards

Lift chest

Bar

Extend body

Land on balls of feet

THE SUPPORT

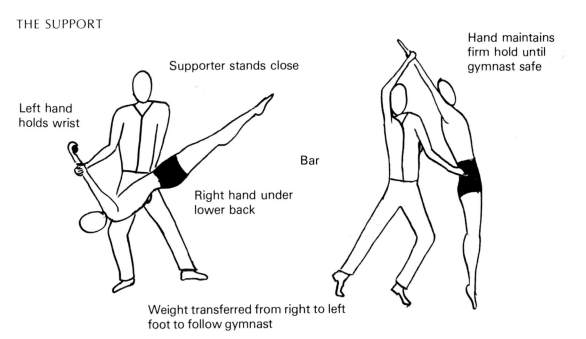

Supporter stands close

Left hand holds wrist

Right hand under lower back

Bar

Hand maintains firm hold until gymnast safe

Weight transferred from right to left foot to follow gymnast

SKILL EXPANSION ACTIVITIES

Because the apparatus is so specific, ie, a beam or a bar, the possibility of 'expanding' the skill is limited to 'hanging' apparatus. (One can not perform the exercise from mats, benches, boxes.) As a consequence the best way of making use of this skill is by varying the starting and finishing positions.

VARIATIONS: 'INS AND OUTS' OF THE UNDERSWING

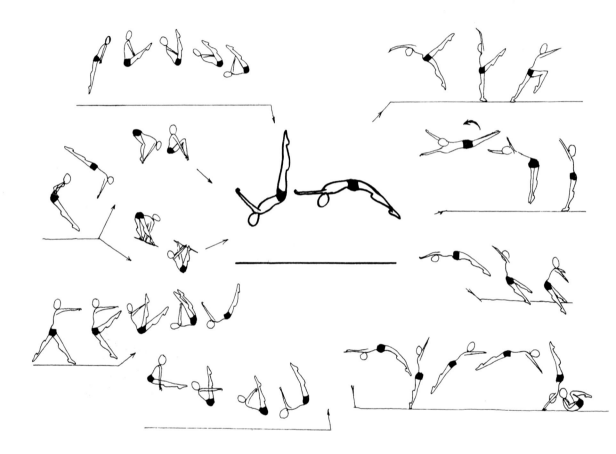

SEQUENCES

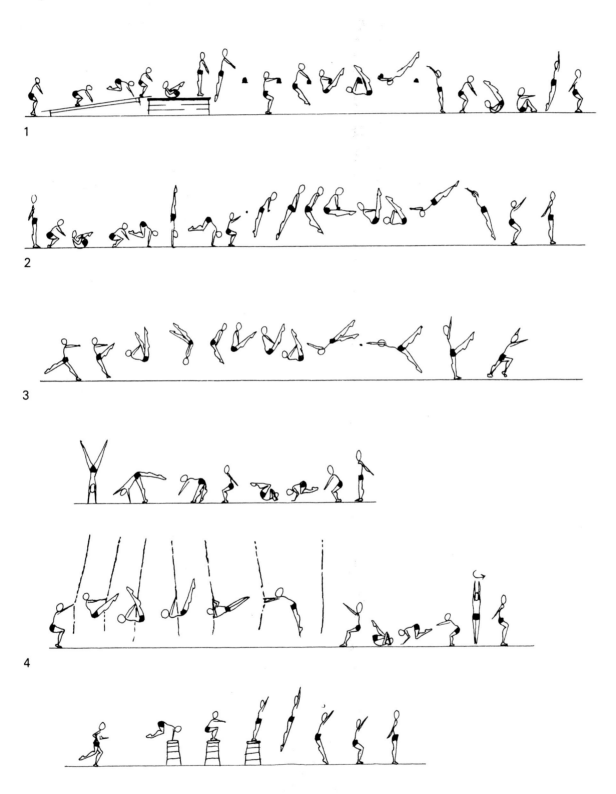

1

2

3

4

The splits and the bridge

Two positions, splits and bridge, have been included in this chapter and treated to a technical examination, as well as a "variations" investigation. It is, however, important to point out a number of considerations which make these particular inclusions somewhat different from the other skills covered.

Apart from a few technical details, such as the position of the back foot in the splits and the direction in which the fingers point in the bridge, there is very little to 'learn'. Pupils will be able to perform them to a degree of competence which will be dictated by the mobility already existing in the joints concerned. To expect all pupils to achieve these positions would be unrealistic, indeed relatively few children will be capable of the splits position and, whilst the bridge will be demonstrated to some degree by most children, good performances will not be the norm. Since some pupils will have the necessary mobility and as these positions are such well known and recognised fundamentals, they can not be legitimately excluded.

THE TECHNIQUE

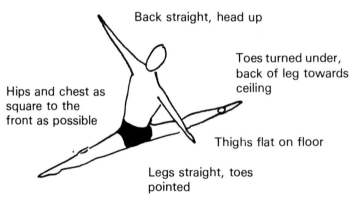

Back straight, head up

Toes turned under, back of leg towards ceiling

Hips and chest as square to the front as possible

Thighs flat on floor

Legs straight, toes pointed

Legs straight and together

Arms straight shoulder width apart

Feet together

Shoulders over or past hands

VARIATIONS: THE 'INS AND OUTS' OF THE
BRIDGE

VARIATIONS: THE 'INS AND OUTS' OF THE SPLITS

The double-foot take-off jump

Whilst an alternative type of gymnastic competition suitable for school use has been suggested in Chapter six there is still a great demand nationally for a standard vaulting and floorwork format. Indeed, within most school gym clubs, whether working on BAGA Awards/inter-school competitions or not, vaulting remains a very common activity. As a consequence this book would be incomplete if we did not examine the technique and teaching method for the double-foot take-off jump which is usually performed from a springboard or reuther board.

The most common difficulty found with this activity is that of co-ordinating the initial hurdle step with the jump itself, ie, one foot jump to two footed jump. The activities illustrated may be used to teach and develop the correct action. The arm swing, where the arms swing from behind the trunk, is an important feature of an efficient and effective jump and should be stressed from the start.

ORIENTATION ACTIVITIES

THE TECHNIQUE

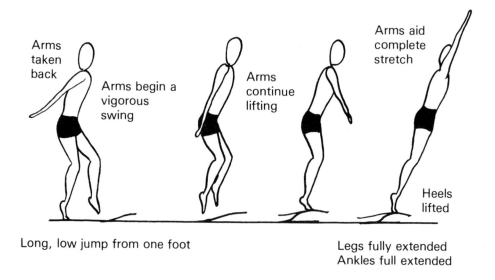

Arms taken back

Arms begin a vigorous swing

Arms continue lifting

Arms aid complete stretch

Heels lifted

Long, low jump from one foot

Legs fully extended
Ankles full extended

SKILL EXPANSION ACTIVITIES

SEQUENCES

1

2

3

4

The straddle vault

ORIENTATION ACTIVITIES

THE TECHNIQUE

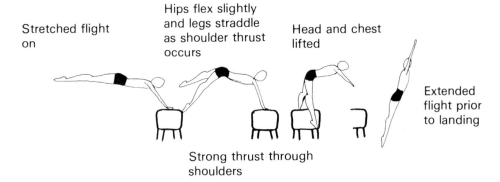

Stretched flight on

Hips flex slightly and legs straddle as shoulder thrust occurs

Head and chest lifted

Extended flight prior to landing

Strong thrust through shoulders

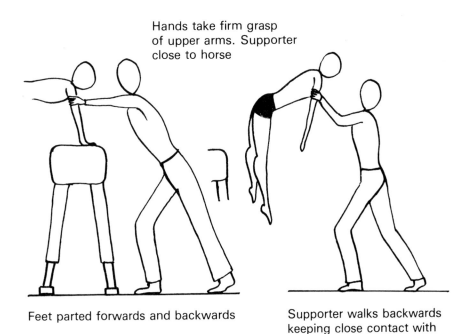

Hands take firm grasp of upper arms. Supporter close to horse

Feet parted forwards and backwards

Supporter walks backwards keeping close contact with performer

The partner activity illustrated is ideal for the teaching of the correct supporting technique to children. Groups of three can work together to gain a competence which may then be transferred to other vaulting situations.

SKILL EXPANSION ACTIVITIES

SEQUENCES

1.

2.

3.

4.

The trampette

The trampette has a great deal to offer teachers of gymnastics. It is a very useful teaching aid and, when correctly used, can add a new dimension to the scope and amplitude of many different skills. Children enjoy using this apparatus but in the early stages are unaware of its potential danger. Teachers who intend to use the trampette, especially as an instrument for skill expansion activities, should ensure that the children receive training in its use before attempting any of the more flighted skills such as vaulting or high jumping.

Throughout the book the reader will be able to pick out occasions in which the trampette is used as a teaching aid. Below are illustrated a few graded activities which could be used to teach the correct and safe use of the apparatus.

ORIENTATION ACTIVITIES

THE TECHNIQUE

Controlled approach run

Arms behind body

Arms start to swing forward

Hurdle step

Arms swing high

Body fully extended

Trampette allowed to project the body

Controlled landing

Some safety rules

1 Ensure that the apparatus is in good condition and especially that:
   (i) the nylon covering on the cables is not badly frayed nor the rubber cord within the covering broken;
   (ii) the supporting leg strut springs are efficient and not over stretched;
   (iii) the bed is evenly tensioned, ie, one side cable is not tighter than the others;
   (iv) the leg strut adjusting screws are secure.
2 The metal frame must be protected with padding. The frame pads which cover the cables and leave the bed exposed are best.

NOTE: Frame pads not shown but must be used

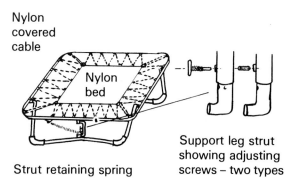

Nylon covered cable

Nylon bed

Strut retaining spring

Support leg strut showing adjusting screws – two types

3 It should be clearly understood that the trampette is only to be used with the teacher's permission.
4 Children should not work from the trampette in stocking feet. Nylon socks tend to slip on the nylon trampette bed.
5 Children should be encouraged to develop the potential of the apparatus slowly and well within their ability to control its effects.
6 Recklessness should never be mistaken for courage, and horseplay should be forbidden.
7 Concentration should be totally on the intended skill as distractions are dangerous.
8 There must always be adequate matting for landings.

If the teacher ensures that the apparatus is in good condition and that safety rules become habitual with the children, then a good deal of benefit will be derived from the use of the trampette.

Supporting gymnastic movements

It is important at the outset to understand the need for support by a teacher or coach during the exercise of a gymnastic movement. There are three important functions to be evaluated when using or constructing a supporting technique to
1 ensure the safety of a performer;
2 give confidence to a performer and eliminate the element of fear;
3 ensure the correct movement paths and direct effort.

It is the intention to take each of these functions and discuss them individually, although it should be understood that there is usually an interdependence of any one on the other two

Safety

There is always the possibility when a new move is being attempted for the first time that complete breakdown may occur. Consequently the main consideration should be safety. It is vitally important that the teacher should fully understand the movement and the most likely places of breakdown. Armed with this knowledge the teacher is in a position to construct a supporting technique which can offer maximum cover for all contingencies. Apart from this obvious aspect of safety there is another consideration to note during the first few attempts at a new movement. We are refering to the judgement of the timing of a contact, regrasp or support shock. Indeed, this problem may persist for some time when familiarity with the correct action is being 'grooved'. Inaccurate assessment of
(i) the forces involved,
(ii) when the shock is to take place,
(iii) the correct body shape to receive the shock, may lead to strains, sprains or worse, if suitable assistance is not given.

It is important, then, that the teacher be aware of the possible consequences following a regrasp or support position made with the body incorrectly shaped for the movement. For example, if the shoulders are well forward of the hands when contact with the floor is made during the performance of the flic-flac, then the teacher should not expect the gymnast to support the weight of his/her body during the final phase of the movement. A suitable lifting assistance will be required if the performer is not to collapse forward onto his/her head.

Confidence

Total commitment to the movement by the performer will only occur if the performer feels the situation to be a safe one. That is to say that the gymnast must feel 'free' and convinced that, whatever happens, no hurt or injury will occur. This is usually a two way process. A teacher, confident in his abilities to handle any possible breakdown, will transmit this confidence to the gymnast who, in turn, will feel confidence in the teacher and will thus be able to think totally about the action that he is about to make, unhampered by anxieties over personal safety. In this context a teacher who is inwardly unsure but outwardly brash could be a liability.

Nothing evaporated a performer's trust in a teacher faster than a mishap due to poor or over ambitious supporting, particularly when the mishap involves some physical pain to the performer. On the other hand nothing strengthens a performer's trust in a teacher more than when he/she is safely brought out of a situation in which he/she was totally 'lost' or out of control. We do not mean to suggest, by this last remark, that the teacher should deliberately expose a gymnast to a potentially dangerous situation in which there is a high probability of this taking place. The gymnast will respect a coach much more for a controlled and knowledgable build up through related stages towards a difficult skill, so that the skill is learned through a gradual expansion of the experience, rather than a heavily supported, long term practice of the complete movement. Apart from the development of the teacher/gymnast relationship within the working situation a gradual build up ensures much more solid mastery of the final skill. Even in the cases where gradual build up is inappropriate or not possible, the teacher must ensure that the previous gymnastic experience of the pupil has been thorough enough to ensure the high probability of success, with support, on the first attempt, or very soon afterwards. In any event even total breakdown of the first attempt must be completed without hurt to the performer.

Effort direction

Once a gymnast has started to become familiar with the skill that he is learning, and is performing the skill safely with minimum support, then the nature of the support can change in emphasis from 'safety' to correctly directing effort. Put simply this means that the coach lets the gymnast supply more and more of the required effort whilst he ensures that the effort goes in the right direction. For example, when coaching a flic-flac the teacher virtually does the movement for the gymnast as the primary barrier to the learning of this skill is the element of fear. After a number of attempts this fear decreases as the performer gains more confidence. Usually the action of the gymnast directs the effort upwards from a position of balance. The teacher must therefore ensure that the effort is directed correctly, ie, backwards, until this becomes familiar. This effort directing function of supporting can also be demonstrated in the later stages of the teaching of the underswing dismount (see page 60). To achieve good flight the gymnast has to allow the hips to swing upwards before extending the body. A teacher could support in such a way that the hips are directed to the correct extension position.

Whilst the provision of strong support, particularly in the effort direction aspect, can speed up the learning process, care should be taken as it may also have an inhibiting effect if over used. Manual support may interfere with proprioceptor feedback and eventually the performer must learn to hold or assume a correct position by relying on information from his/her own sense receptors. If the need for manual support persists then a teacher should examine the effectiveness of his earlier build up practices. It is possible that insufficient time was given to them.

In conclusion, teachers or coaches need to establish *why* he/she is offering support to a gymnast in order that the question of *how* to support can be answered satisfactorily.

CHAPTER THREE

Class organisation, lesson planning and schemes of work

Aims and objectives

The purpose of teaching is, of course, to assist in the learning process. To a large extent, the efficiency and effectiveness of teaching will depend upon a teacher's clear understanding of his aims and objectives. It is proposed therefore to clarify the meaning of these terms and to provide a guideline for their application in the planning of lessons and schemes of work.

Aims are general expressions of intent which may be long or short term. They should be purposeful, explicit statements that act as a guide for a teacher's strategy. Thus a long term aim might be

– to promote interest and enthusiasm in physical education and sport by achieving success in acquiring gymnastic skills.

Aims may also be short term, eg

– to help the pupils understand the importance of variety when performing floor routines.

The success of a teacher's aims necessarily involves reviewing the outcomes over a period of time. In the long term example given it could be a question of years before any measure of its success might be estimated. In the short term aim, however, it may only be a question of weeks before the outcomes are evident. In any event the fulfilment of a teaching aim is not a matter of an immediate response or result. How appropriate or useful any particular aim might be, can be partly judged by the number of objectives that can be derived from it. Clearly then, an aim should contain certain matters of substance.

Objectives, which should be based on aims, are much more specific and directly related to the planning of individual lessons. Objectives, however, may be categorised into *behavioural* and *non-behavioural*. Behavioural objectives are concerned with identifiable outcomes, for example,

– the pupils will perform orientation activities related to the cartwheel.

Thus the behavioural objective will be manifested in an observable form, ie movement. Non-behavioural objectives do not produce readily observable changes in behaviour but may refer more to what the teacher intends to do, elements of content and less tangible factors such as appreciation, for example,

– to help the children appreciate the importance of height at take-off.

Such non-behavioural objectives are none-the-less important but clearly not readily quantifiable. However, care should be taken that in any single lesson a balance between behavioural and non-behavioural objectives is achieved. The teaching of gymnastic skills is principally associated with producing specific outcomes. We are therefore largely concerned with formulating behavioural objectives that are demonstrated overtly as a result of teacher guidance.

Because objectives are specific they are concerned with immediate effect, for example,

– to teach the core skill of the handspring.

The statement is quite clear and unambiguous, the objectives state exactly what a teacher is trying to achieve in this lesson. Furthermore, whether he is successful in achieving this objective will be evident by the end of the lesson. In other words the pupils, or the majority of the pupils, will be able or unable to perform a handspring.

To summarise, aims are general expressions of intent that may be either long or short term. Objectives, on the other hand, are specific and may be behavioural or non-behavioural. They are intimately related to the individual lesson and do not necessarily require inclusion in schemes of work. Equally, aims do not need to be re-stated at the outset of each lesson plan. In the final analysis, a teacher ought to be able to judge the success of this *educational intent* against his stated aims and objectives. The relationship between aims, objectives, schemes of work and lesson plans is illustrated by the model below.

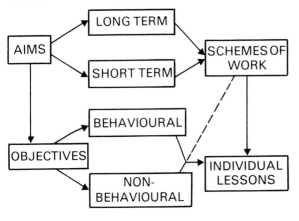

Class organisation

In order to help children to acquire skills they should be given ample opportunity to practise. Accordingly, most lessons should include sections when new skills or activities are introduced and when previously taught skills can be practised. The suggested format, therefore, for a traditional gymnastics lesson is that shown below:

1 Introductory activities – Warm up activities and body preparation activities.
2 Skill development – Class activity work on specific skills or activities.
3 Group practice – Practice in order to develop and retain previously taught skills.

Introductory activities

These should involve the large muscle groups and should be progressively strenuous. Since the mechanically correct and efficient acquisition of gymnastic skills requires a good degree of flexibility, time should be given to body preparation activities (see Appendix A). Wherever possible, warm-up activities should be related to the skills which the children will be practising at a later stage in the lesson. If the class activity part of the lesson is based, for example, on the through vault, useful warm-up activities would be running and jumping from two feet to a tucked position in the air. It is important that all the children are active at the outset. It is generally inappropriate to include relay type activities where one child works whilst the others in the group wait for their turn. Since many gymnastic

skills involve weight being taken on hands and the body passing through inverted positions, the practice of handstands, cartwheels and combinations of these two often make useful warm-up activities. The inclusion of a few activities which are amusing and enjoyable can also be appropriate. They may help to motivate and set an atmosphere which encourages hard work on the various skills they are trying to acquire (see Appendix A).

Skill development

This part of the lesson involves either the introduction of new skills, related skill expansion activities or variations of a previously taught core skill. It is usually carried out as a class activity with all the children working at their own level on a core skill or modification of a core skill to suit individual children. This part of the lesson should involve the children working on a particular skill or skills for at least ten to fifteen minutes.

Group practice

Group practice should account for the majority of lesson time. At least 20 minutes should be given to working on previously taught skills in order to acquire them, or retain a high level of proficiency. Children enjoy repeating skills they have acquired and they should be given the opportunity to do so for both motivational and skill retention reasons. During the lesson children should work in small groups of approximately five and rotate from one piece of apparatus to another. A simple workable system based on introducing new skills as a class activity then putting that skill into the group practice part of the lesson in subsequent weeks is outlined below. Since children may have no previous experience of taught specific skills, the system shown below indicates how the group work can be built up until new skills are continually moving into the system and old ones move out or become part of the individual sequence.

Lesson 1
(i)   Class activity work on skill A.
(ii) Class activity work on skill B.

Lesson 2
(i)   Class activity work on skill C.
(ii) *Group practice:* 6 groups of 5 boys
        3 groups practising skill A initially,
        3 groups practising skill B initially

Lesson 3
(i)   Class activity on skill D.
(ii) *Group practice:*
        2 groups practising skill A initially,
        2 groups practising skill B initially,
        2 groups practising skill C initially

Lesson 4
(i)   Class activity work on skill E
(ii) *Group practice:*
        1 group practising skill A initially,
        1 group practising skill B initially,
        2 groups practising skill C initially,
        2 groups practising skill D initially

Lesson 5
(i)   Class activity work on skill F
(ii) *Group practice:*
        1 group practising skill A initially,
        1 group practising skill B initially,
        1 group practising skill C initially,
        1 group practising skill D initially,
        2 groups practising skill E initially

Lesson 6
(i)   Class activity work on skill G
(ii) *Group practice:*
        1 group practising skill A initially,
        1 group practising skill B initially,
        1 group practising skill C initially,
        1 group practising skill D initially,
        1 group practising skill E initially,
        1 group practising skill F initially

Lesson 7
(i)   Class activity work on skill H
(ii) *Group practice:*
        1 group practising skill B initially,
        1 group practising skill C initially,
        1 group practising skill D initially,
        1 group practising skill E initially,
        1 group practising skill F initially,
        1 group practising skill G initially

By this lesson the initial skill taught (skill A) has dropped out of the system. As new skills are introduced in subsequent lessons, so skills taught earlier are no longer included unless it is incorporated into a sequence.

The above plan indicates that time is always given to class activity work and group practice. However, it is not necessary to follow this rigidly. A teacher may decide, for example, to introduce a core skill and spend the remainder of the lesson on skill expansion activities. It is also possible that a teacher may be timetabled for short single period lessons allowing for as little as 20 minutes working time. Accordingly, he may decide to spend one lesson entirely on a core skill and a few selected variations and the next entirely on group practice of previously taught skills. It could be inferred from the plan that different core skills must be introduced each lesson. This again is not necessary. Skill A in lesson one, for example, may be the forward roll and two or three selected variations. Skill E could be further work on the forward roll with new variations being introduced to the children. It is also desirable that a lesson, or part of a lesson, be used from time to time to develop individual sequences. The teaching of specific gymnastic skills requires considerable fore-thought in the positioning of apparatus in order to avoid loss of working time. It will often be necessary to arrange apparatus for a class activity session and then re-arrange it for group work. A teacher should bear in mind that during group practice, the children should rotate to a different type of apparatus each time, for example, from boxes to mats to beams.

Planning the content

The content of a syllabus and lessons arising from it should be carefully planned. Many factors including the children's previous experience, the size of the class, time and the apparatus available, as well as the teacher's own philosophy, will influence the final outcome. In order to assist teachers planning a syllabus two approaches are discussed below. The first approach assumes that there are certain constraints on time and equipment. In this case the syllabus suggested comprises mainly of a number of core skills and their variations. Lessons arising from the syllabus would normally have the objectives of helping the children acquire a number of these skills and develop a routine.

This approach may be preferred by physical education students since it is relatively straightforward.

The other approach discussed is a more comprehensive programme of gymnastics. Whilst the syllabus is still based on the teaching of core skills and variations, each of the skills is fully developed through a variety of skill expansion activities. With more time available teachers should also consider the inclusion of body preparation activities. These will help children develop flexibility and strength and enable them to acquire skills more easily as well as increasing their potential range. Obviously teacher is not faced with just the choice of implementing either the introductory programme or the more comprehensive one. A compromise can be made by selecting certain skills and fully developing these through skill expansion activities. Other skills and variations may be introduced, but not fully developed, through the exploration of many different situations and pieces of apparatus on which these skills can be practised.

An introductory programme

In this approach basic core skills are introduced to the children as a class activity. An attempt is made immediately to develop sound technique. The problem of coping with a wide range of ability can be overcome by selecting situations which require high or low levels of competence. Various ability levels will in fact be reflected in the wide range of performance levels achieved. Accordingly, a teacher should aim to have children perform the skill to the best of their ability. Good timing and perfect technique should be encouraged with the more able. The less able should be encouraged to complete the skill successfully and to improve on their technique with successive attempts. A sound knowledge of correct technique is essential since a teacher may have to modify the core skill for a few children who are having difficulty performing the basic move. Following the teaching of the core skill, the related variations can be introduced. It is usually possible for many of these to be introduced as a class activity. However, during this stage a teacher should concentrate on helping children develop variations, often of their own choosing, appropriate to their ability level. The more able should be asked to perform challenging variations which demand hard work and concentration in order to be successful. The

less able should be guided towards variations which, whilst demanding comparative degrees of effort and co-ordination, are suited to their individual ability levels.

Simply by walking around the class and carefully observing the children working a teacher can quickly give instructions to individual children, asking them to modify the starting and finishing positions or add to the basic skill they are practising. A teacher may introduce, for example, forward roll to straddle. Whilst the children are practising he may suggest that one pupil rolls to sit with legs astride because this individual may not have the flexibility to regain his feet. Another pupil who quickly acquires this skill can be asked to start in a handstand or follow the straddle roll with a headstand.

Since many of the core skills shown earlier have numerous variations, it may be inadvisable to introduce one of these skills and subsequently teach all of the possible variations over the next few weeks. The programme should show a degree of variety. The forward roll and a few variations may, for example, be taught over two lessons. The next few lessons may centre on another core skill in order to show some variety before returning to the forward roll to explore further variations and developments. To take a core skill and in subsequent lessons try to explore all the possible variations and skill expansion activities could well be a receipt for tedium. The number of consecutive lessons devoted to developing a core skill will depend on the nature of the skill involved. More than two or three lessons with class activity work based on the forward roll may be too many. However, the cartwheel with its orientation activities and moves into and out of the cartwheel could easily be developed over a number of consecutive lessons and still provide challenging and exciting work for the pupils.

It should be remembered that it is important for each child to develop his own sequence. This should be done with assistance from the teacher. Accordingly, class activity work for some lessons should be based on an examination of the main principles of sequence development. Certain movements which link well together should be examined and used as examples in order to explain the importance of continuity, variety, etc. The short scheme of work and lesson plans following are based on the straightforward approach under discussion. The assumption is made that the children have no previous experience of being taught specific gymnastic skills with teacher using a direct teaching approach. Consequently, during the first few lessons it is not possible to place the children in groups working on different skills. However, by lesson seven, sufficient skills have been introduced for this to operate. As each new skill is introduced so the vocabulary of core skills increases.

Sample scheme of work based on an introductory approach to the teaching of gymnastic skills

AIMS

1 To introduce and develop a number of core skills.
2 To develop an understanding of basic principles related to a good performance of gymnastic skills.
3 To help children develop an understanding of the fundamental concepts related to the construction of a good routine.

CONTENT

The content is listed as units of work since for certain core skills teachers may decide to spend more than one lesson on introducing a skill and its related variations. For example, unit 8 may be taught over two lessons. It may not be possible to teach some of the core skills as a class activity due to a lack of sufficient apparatus. Units 5 and 10, for example, may take the form of a group practice lesson throughout. The teacher would position himself at the beam. The groups would rotate throughout the lesson. Each group in turn would then receive teaching from the teacher on the particular beam skills.

Unit 1
An introduction to
   (i)   Forward rolls
  (ii) Squat on, jump off horse

Unit 2
Class activity: Backward rolls
Group practice: Six groups of five boys
   (i)   Squat on, jumps off
  (ii) Forward rolls

Unit 3
Class activity: Through vault
Group practice: Six groups of five boys
   (i)   Backward rolls
  (ii) Squat on, jumps off
 (iii) Forward rolls

Unit 4
Class activity: Running jumps into place
Group practice: Six groups of five boys
   (i)   Through vault
  (ii) Backward rolls
 (iii) Squat on, jumps off
 (iv) Forward rolls

Unit 5
Class activity: Beam traverses
Group practice: Six groups of five boys
   (i)   Running jumps
  (ii) Through vaults
 (iii) Backward rolls
 (iv) Squat on, jumps off
  (v) Forward rolls

Unit 6
Class activity: Headstand
Group Practice: Six groups of five boys
   (i)   Beam traverses
  (ii) Jumps
 (iii) Through vaults
 (iv) Backward rolls
  (v) Squat on, jumps off
 (vi) Forward rolls

Unit 7
Class activity: Handstand
Group practice: Six groups of five boys
   (i)   Headstand
  (ii) Beam traverses
 (iii) Jumps
 (iv) Through vault
  (v) Backward rolls
 (vi) Squat on, jumps off

Unit 8

Class activity: Cartwheel
Group practice: Six groups of five boys
   (i)   Handstand
   (ii) Headstand
   (iii) Beam traverse
   (iv) Jumps
   (v) Through vault
   (vi) Backward rolls

Unit 9

Class activity: Developing a sequence
No group work.

Unit 10

Class activity: Upward circle (beam or bar)
Group practice:
   (i)   Cartwheel
   (ii) Handstand
   (iii) Headstand
   (iv) Beam traverse
   (v) Jumps
   (vi) Through vault

Unit 11

Class activity: Construct and practise individual sequences
No group work.

Sample lesson plan

This lesson plan is based on unit seven of the above scheme of work. It requires a fair amount of working time. If less than 40 minutes are available it may be better to expand the class activity part and teach it as one lesson. The group practice will then form the basis of the next lessons.

It is not necessary to include detailed teaching points for each of the group practice activities since each one has been the subject of class activity work in previous lessons. The teaching points, therefore, may be found by referring back to the appropriate lesson plan.

OBJECTIVES

BEHAVIOURAL

1 To help the children acquire skills related to the handstand.
   (i)   hand balance on elbow
   (ii) handstand against the wall facing both towards and away from the wall
   (iii) handstand with a partner
   (iv) supporting a partner in handstand
   (v) variations to suit the ability level of individuals finding the core skill either too easy or too difficult.
2 To give pupils the opportunity to retain and improve their performance of the previously introduced skills of the headstand, beam traverse, running jumps, through vault, backward rolls, squat on, jumps off (broad horse).

NON-BEHAVIOURAL

1 To help the pupils appreciate the principles of balancing on the hands.
2 To recap on principles related to the acquisition of skills taught earlier.

Activity	Teaching points	Organisation
1 Running, tuck jumps, straddle jumps	Encourage strenuous activity with good height and style in the jumps	Pupils working individually
2 Weight onto hands, kick legs in the air	Stay on the hands as long as possible	

Class activity

1 Balance on hands, knees and elbows	Hands shoulder width apart, rock hips over to shoulders to balance	
2 Handstand against the wall	Explain and demonstrate the skill. Hands shoulder width apart	Pupils working individually on mats placed against the wall
(a) facing the wall	approximately 30 cm from the wall	
(b) facing outwards	Climb the legs up the wall and simultaneously move the hands inwards and the legs higher. Practice kicking away from the wall to find the balanced position on the hands, push back with the fingers	Pupils in pairs. Partners prevent the performer overbalancing
3 Handstand with support	Demonstrate the supporting technique, foot to be placed between the performers hands, knees against shoulder. Hands reach for the hips as performer kicks up. In the balanced position the performers legs should rest against the supporters shoulders	In pairs on mats

4 Handstand variations (to individuals finding the core skill too easy or too difficult) eg

Easy skills:
(i) one hand one foot
(ii) one foot two hands

More advanced skills:
(i) two foot jump to handstand
(ii) straddle lift to handstand

Group practice

1 Headstand	Details of technique may be	Six groups of five pupils
2 Beam traverse	found in previous lesson plans.	
3 Running jumps with a roll	Pupils have been introduced	
4 Through vault	to a few variations of each	
5 Backward rolls (mats)	of these skills. Accordingly,	
6 Squat on – jumps off	they should practise	
	acquiring skills appropriate	
	to their ability level	

Conclusion
After the apparatus has been
put away pupils should
practise handstands in pairs

A developmental programme

In order to reach a full developmental programme, a teacher must ensure a regular timetable commitment to the teaching of gymnastic skills. The approach is fundamentally the same as for the introductory one described above except that the skills are more fully developed by practising a number of skill expansion activities. This applies not only to core skills but, where appropriate, for a number of variations. The forward roll, for example, may be practised not only on the floor but on benches, boxes and tables. In addition it can also be performed in a variety of situations, over obstacles or over partners. For example, the variations of forward roll straddle, or forward roll quarter turn to knees can then be introduced and each of these variations can in turn be expanded by practising them in a variety of situations. The core skill is thus well developed leading to children practising and acquiring a considerable number of specific skills and developing the ability to create and master variations.

The acquisition of more complex skills can be assisted by practising orientation activities. If a full commitment is being made to the teaching of gymnastics these may be included as class activity work prior to a lesson on the specific skill. For example, if a handspring is to be introduced as a core skill to a group of children, a teacher may well spend the initial lesson in a range of simple activities which contain aspects of the fundamental 'feeling' concepts of the handspring (see 'Orientation activities', page 49).

To facilitate the acquisition of a wide range of skills, children need a degree of flexibility and strength. Suitable exercises for physical preparation should be taught and practised during the warm-up and/or concluding activities. Examples of these are included in Appendix 'A'. The scheme of work suggested below includes a number of skill expansion activities in addition to core skills and their variations. Each core skill can provide material for a number of lessons. Care must be taken, however, not to teach one core skill and its related variations and skill expansion activities for too long. Since numerous skills are often involved, the scheme should allow for work on other skills to be dovetailed.

Sample scheme of work forming part of a developmental programme for the teaching of gymnastic skills

AIMS

1 An introduction to the core skills of the cartwheel and the headstand.
2 To develop a full range of variations and skill expansion activities based on the core skill of the cartwheel and the headstand.
3 To provide opportunities for practising and developing –
   (a) previously taught skills, and
   (b) a floor sequence.

CONTENT

Using a developmental programme, children are introduced to a wide range of skills on a variety of apparatus. Accordingly, during the 'group practice' section of a lesson, the children should be encouraged to practise the core skills and their variations which are applicable to the apparatus being used. This approach will allow the children to develop previously taught skills without being too restrictive.

Unit 1

Class activity: An introduction to the cartwheel through orientation activities
Group practice:
1 Floor routine
2 Beam – upstarts to gain a position above the beam
3 Mats – balances
4 Broad horse – vaults
5 Beam – dismounts
6 Long horse – squat on, vault off

Unit 2

Class activity: Teaching the technique of the core skill – the cartwheel
Group practice:
1 Floor routine
2 Beam – upstarts
3 Mats – balances
4 Broad horse – vaults
5 Beam – dismounts
6 Long horse – squat on, vault off

Unit 3

Class activity: Skill expansion activities based on the cartwheel
Group practice:
1 Floor routine
2 Beam – upstarts
3 Mats – balances
4 Broad horse – vaults
5 Beam – dismounts
6 Long horse – squat on, vault off

Unit 4

Class activity: The headstand introduced through orientation activities
Group practice:
1 Floor routine
2 Beam – upstarts
3 Mats – cartwheels
4 Broad horse – vaults
5 Beam – dismounts
6 Long horse – squat on, vault off

Unit 5

Class activity: The headstand – teaching the technique of the core skill
Group practice:
1 Floor routine
2 Beam – upstarts
3 Mats – cartwheels
4 Broad horse – vaults
5 Beam – dismounts
6 Long horse – squat on, vault off

Unit 6

Class activity: Skill expansion activities based on the headstand

Group practice:
1 Floor routine
2 Beam – upstarts
3 Mats – cartwheels
4 Broad horse – vaults
5 Beam – dismounts
6 Long horse – squat on, vault off

Unit 7

Class activity: Cartwheel variations and moves into and out of the cartwheel

Group pratice:
1 Mats – headstands
2 Long horse – squat on, vault off
3 Floor routine
4 Beam – upstarts
5 Broad horse – vaults
6 Beam – dismounts

Unit 8

Class activity: Skill expansion activities based on variations of the cartwheel

Group practice:
1 Mats – headstands
2 Long horse – squat on, vaults off
3 Beam – upstarts
4 Floor routine incorporating the cartwheel/variations
5 Broad horse – vaults
6 Beam – dismounts

Unit 9

Class activity: The 'ins and outs' of the headstand (variations)

Group practice:
1 Mats – floor routine incorporating balances and cartwheels
2 Long horse, squat on vaults off
3 Beam – upstarts
4 Floor routine incorporating the cartwheel and variations
5 Broad horse – vaults
6 Beam – dismounts

Unit 10

Class activity: Skill expansion activities based on variations of the headstand

Group practice:
1 Mats – floor routine incorporating balances and cartwheels
2 Long horse, squat on, vaults off.

3 Beam – upstarts
4 Floor routine incorporating the cartwheel and variations
5 Broad horse – vaults
6 Beam – dismounts

Unit 11

Class activity: The routine:– using some of the skills practised during the previous 7 units each child now creates a sequence which must incorporate a cartwheel and a headstand together with a variation of each of the skills.

Apparatus and mats to be placed around the gymnasium (with consideration being given to safety) so that the children may move freely constructing and practising their sequences
No group work

Sample lesson plan based on the developmental approach

The lesson shown requires a fair amount of working time to be available, at least 40 minutes. This would be necessary in view of the time required to set up apparatus for the class activity and the group work. If less time is available it may be better to teach the class activity work in one lesson and the group work in a subsequent one.

BEHAVIOURAL OBJECTIVES

1 To help children acquire the skill of the through vault.
2 To organise a group practice session to allow for further practice of:
   (a) cartwheels
   (b) squat on, vault off the long horse
   (c) upstarts and dismounts on the beam
   (d) squat on, vault off the long horse
   (e) floor routine
   (f) beam traverse

NON BEHAVIOURAL OBJECTIVES

1 To help the children to understand the principles related to successful performance of the through vault.
2 To re-cap on principles related to the successful performance of previously taught skills.

Activity	Teaching points	Organisation
Introduction		
1 Running freely, practising tucked jumps	Take off two feet, gain as much height as possible. Tight tucked position. Use arms to assist lift. Resilient landing	Children moving freely around the gymnasium
2 From front support jump to squat position	Draw knees up quickly. Thrust out from shoulders. As much time as possible between hands leaving and the feet contacting	Individual practice
Class activity:		
1 *The through vault*		
(a) Jump to crouch on the apparatus	1 Explanation and demonstration of the whole skill on the broad horse (a) Demo of two foot take-off and the crouch position. Try to push off hands so that they are extended forward before feet land on box	Children work in six groups on apparatus shown in diagram
(b) Supporting technique	(b) Demonstration of the technique. Ensure that support is taken early and firmly. Keep firm hold until action fully completed	Children practise in groups of 4 as illustrated at the foot of page 45
(c) Practice of the through vault	(c) Two foot take-off. Push off hands. Tuck knees up tightly	Children move from piece to piece freely, choosing apparatus appropriate to ability level. Initial attempts on each apparatus to be supported
Group practice:		
1 The cartwheel	For details of the technique see previous lesson plans. Practice core skill followed by variations, when core skill reaches competent level	Children work in their six groups and rotate groups in turn

2 Squat on, vault off (Long horse)	As above
3 Upstarts and dismounts (Beam)	Practice previously taught skills
4 Squat on, jump off (Broad horse)	4 Practice variations of jump off
5 Floor routine	5 Routine to contain at least six moves including a cartwheel
6 Beam traverses	6 Practice various methods taught

Conclusion: After apparatus cleared – free practice of handstands and cartwheels.

Diagrams of apparatus layout

1. CLASS ACTIVITY ON THROUGH VAULT

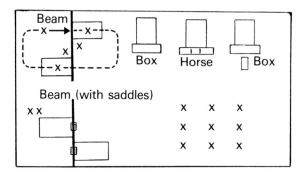

2. GROUP PRACTICE

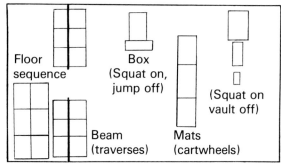

CHAPTER FOUR

The learning and performance of gymnastic skills

In Chapter One we outlined an approach to teaching and coaching gymnastics. Also we attempted to show how those teaching strategies proposed are related to theoretical aspects of skills acquisition. The aim of this chapter is both to examine the concepts involved and also to show how different emphasis is placed on these aspects. It is outside the scope of this book to examine the various concepts in any real depth and there is the danger then of presenting complex issues in an over simplified manner. However, we hope that the chapter will serve as a useful introduction and encourage readers to study some of the more theoretical texts to which we have referred. The study of skills acquisition has been made more difficult because of a lack of unanimity in the interpretations of certain concepts and terms. We propose, therefore, to examine some basic concepts before discussing different approaches to skills acquisition.

Skilled performance

Skill is difficult to measure and interpret and many definitions and classifications have weaknesses and omissions. Whiting (1975; 3) pointed out that in classifying some observed behaviour as *skilled*, it is being distinguished from other behaviour which is *unskilled*. Thus, he suggests a continuum *'skilled – unskilled'* is a simple, but useful, way of classifying behaviour. We should be conscious that skill is a relative quality and any attempt to define it in absolute terms will meet with difficulties. A gymnast may be considered very skilful by his peers in the local school club, but the same performer may look relatively unskilled in the English Schools Gymnastics Championships. Clearly, the issue is about levels and standards.

The *skilled – unskilled* continuum is a useful concept but as Whiting pointed out, it may not be appropriate to all behaviour. We need to consider the criteria on which skilled behaviour is assessed if we are to answer questions such as 'what is a skill?' Whiting suggested that three criteria must be met if behaviour is to be described as skilful. It must be learned behaviour and must be both complex and intentional. Skilled behaviour was defined as:

'Complex, intentional actions involving a whole chain of sensory, central and motor mechanisms which through the process of learning have come to be organised in such a way as to achieve predetermined objectives with maximum certainty.'

(Whiting 1975: 6)

Applying this to gymnastics, it can be seen that skill requires a pupil to make a number of appropriate perceptual and motor responses which have been acquired by learning. Possession of Skill in gymnastics enables a person to achieve a particular goal with precision and accuracy. The expert gymnast, for example, will perform a back somersault at shoulder height, showing minimum travel and finishing in a good upright position. The acquisition of a gymnastics skill, then, is a process through which the learner develops a set of motor responses into an integrated and organised movement pattern. Skill is specific and each new task involves a new set of motor responses which must be coordinated to produce the required outcome.

Abilities and skill

Ability and skill are not synonymous and it is important to distinguish their similarities and differences. Sage (1977) provided a clear distinction when he stated that *abilities* serve as foundation stones for the development of *skills* which are specific responses for the accomplishment of a task. A *skill*, eg, a handspring, is learned through practice and depends on the presence of underlying *abilities* such as explosive strength, dynamic flexibility and multi-limb coordination. The structure and measurement of these abilities has been the subject of considerable research. Whiting (1975: 61) discusses the work of Parker who classified eighteen basic perceptual-motor abilities into four categories following his research on performance related to the Gemini mission:

1 Fine manipulative abilities, eg, manual dexterity.
2 Gross positioning and movement abilities, eg, make fine, controlled positioning movements.
3 System equalisation abilities, eg, movement prediction such as the ability to estimate future target position.
4 Perceptual-cognitive abilities, eg, reaction time, the ability to respond as rapidly as possible to a discreet signal.

Fleishman (1964) used statistical techniques to identify the relatively small number of abilities which are utilised in the performance of a skill. He proposed eleven motor abilities that included control precision, multi-limb coordination and reaction time. In addition he postulated nine physical proficiency abilities, including static strength, dynamic strength and dynamic flexibility. The level of performance of a cartwheel, for example, may depend on basic abilities such as multi-limb coordination and trunk strength. It appears that some abilities depend more on genetic than learning factors, but most depend to some degree on both. The rate of learning and ultimate proficiency level depends on the structure of abilities within each individual. Thus each person appears to have certain potentials for learning a skill.

It has been proposed (Singer 1975: 227) that a particular combination of abilities that contribute to motor skill performance can be identified and that changes in the combination of these abilities occur with continued practice and improvement. Early performance of a cartwheel on the long horse may rely on the use of vision as the performer must look in order to judge where to place his hands. During later performances the gymnast seeks to obtain the correct 'feel' of the move. In order to achieve this, he relies on his proprioceptive abilities, such as the ability of the receptors in the muscles to transmit information on the degree of stretch. If the possession of certain abilities at a specific level is vital to the learning of a skill, then it may be a valuable procedure to attempt to develop these abilities prior to the skill being attempted. Thus if a move depends on balance, explosive strength and dynamic flexibility, as in the back somersault on the beam, then these abilities must be developed to a high level prior to attempting to learn the move. Most coaches of elite gymnasts now recognise that specific *abilities* must be developed if their performers are to acquire certain *skills*. Expressed in simple terms this means that a 'plank' will not be able to do a backward walkover until it can bend.

The concept of abilities as foundation blocks for skills has important implications for primary school physical education. If there are a set of underlying abilities from which various combinations are formed in order to perform specific skills then possibly the emphasis should be on developing these abilities in young children. At a later age specific skills can be taught. If the underlying abilities are well developed then skills acquisition should be facilitated. A major problem with implementing this is deciding how much emphasis should be placed on this approach and at what age. It can also be argued that a wide range of specific skills should be taught at an early age, not just for their intrinsic value but for their contribution in developing these underlying abilities. A considerable amount of research must be done before such questions can be fully resolved.

Learning and performance

Learning is a relatively permanent change in behaviour brought about by experience and training. In order to acquire complex gymnastic skills which consist of a number of specific responses we must learn how to make the movement patterns which are involved. In addition we must learn when to make these movements. This is achieved by learning to recognise stimuli and make appropriate responses. This stimuli may be visual, auditory, kinaesthetic or any combination of the various senses. When a gymnast performs a skill or sequence of skills, he may be considered as responding in a certain way to a particular set of stimuli. These responses must be made in a sequential order. The gymnast often responds to stimuli which arise from proprioceptors within the body. During the headspring, for example, the skilled performer, on reaching the correct angled position will receive internal stimuli from muscle spindles, tendon organs and joint receptors which inform him that he has achieved a particular position. This will initiate the second phase, that of throwing the legs over and pushing on the hands. The correct timing of responses is essential for the successful execution of motor skills.

The skilled gymnast has learned a variety of movement patterns which through practice have become automatic. These patterns are stored in unconscious motor memory and released when the appropriate situation occurs. In a handstand, for example, the skilled gymnast automatically pushes back with his fingers if the body begins to overbalance. He may not be consciously aware of his actions, indeed he may be thinking of something else such as the move following the handstand. Responses only become automatic after considerable practice. In the early stages of learning it is necessary to concentrate on the fundamental aspects in order to successfully perform a skill since the brain can only handle a certain amount of information. Teachers and coaches should not give too many coaching points initially. It is usually better to concentrate on one movement pattern at a time, such as placing the hands on the far end of the box in the straddle vault. When this pattern has been acquired, he can then concentrate on developing or improving the next pattern such as the position of the legs.

When a gymnast performs a particular skill it often gives an indication of his skill level. However, this is not always the case and it is important to acknowledge that the level of *learning* and level of *performance* are not identical concepts. Performance may be influenced by factors other than the amount of learning that has taken place. For example, a gymnast who normally performs a front somersault to a high standard may perform badly on one particular occasion through fatigue or a sudden inexplicable fear of injury. Thus his performance would indicate a lower level of learning than was actually the case. The reverse is also true. The author clearly remembers teaching a Yamashita vault to a pupil. After a number of abortive attempts he suddenly produced the almost perfect vault with excellent flight off the box. Sadly, it was never repeated despite numerous attempts he never acquired the skill.

Perception

Psychologically, a fine discrimination is made between the processes of *sensation* and *perception*. Sensation is the reception of stimuli by sense organs. Perception is the act of interpreting the stimuli registering in the brain. The boy who performed one good Yamashita may have perceived the experience considerably differently from a gymnast who frequently performs the move at a high level of skill. Information from the proprioceptors giving an awareness of good height at take off may have caused the novice some anxiety as he approached the ground. The expert, however, may experience a feeling of elation as he knows he has achieved a good take off which will lead to a good vault and safe landing. Perception therefore is a process largely influenced by memories of previous similar situations. In addition, our feelings, attitudes, goals and needs all play a part in determining how we perceive the stimuli which we receive in the brain.

We do not perceive stimuli related to something specific in isolation. Because of our inherent tendency to see things in an organised totality we see them in a setting. What we are concentrating on is referred to as 'the figure', the rest of the information is referred to as 'the ground'. In any given situation there is too much stimuli to attend to. We therefore selectively attend to just some of the stimuli available. Learning to selectively attend to relevant stimuli and ignore irrelevant stimuli plays an important role in the acquisition of sports skills. The expert makes relevant stimuli 'the figure'. Irrelevant information becomes 'the ground'. In the floor exercise in a gymnastics competition, for example, the expert can 'block out' noise from the crowd and concentrate on how he is performing his routine. This information is provided by his proprioceptors which inform him of his movement patterns. The novice, on the other hand, may be distracted by the crowd. By attending to their noise he will be less able to attend to the stimuli arising from his proprioceptors. He is therefore more likely to make performance errors in his routine.

Perception along with memory, imagination and thinking composes the cognitive processes. These processes have received increasing attention in recent years with the development of the *'information processing'* approach to the study of skills acquisition. This approach is examined later in this chapter.

Feedback

Feedback refers to the information which the individual receives from his performance which enables him to profit from the experience. Thus subsequent attempts at a skill are based on feedback information gained from previous attempts and stored in the memory. A skilful gymnast will know from previous experience that he can only regain his feet in the standing back somersault if he avoids leaning back excessively on take off. Accordingly he will make a concerted effort to take off almost vertically, particularly if in earlier attempts, excessive lean backwards resulted in poor landings. Feedback has three functions. It is a source of information, it may motivate people and it may provide reinforcement. In the early stages of learning feedback shapes responses.

Feedback information is available both during and after the performance of a skill. During the floor exercise, for example, a highly skilled gymnast makes continual almost automatic readjustments in motor responses. These adjustments are made as a result of receiving information from the proprioceptors, ie muscle spindles, tendon organs and joint receptors. The monitoring of a skilled gymnastic performance through proprioception is largely unconscious. Once a skill has been mastered, any attempt to pay conscious attention to the details of the move may have a disrupting effect.

The performance of many gymnastic skills supply intrinsic feedback during and/or immediately after a response is made. If a gymnast kicks up too slowly in the handstand, for example, he becomes aware of this during the move as the legs slow down before reaching the balanced position on the hands. At the end of the attempt he is aware of the failure and may kick up the legs harder for the next attempt. The performance of some skills may not provide the gymnast with sufficient intrinsic feedback in order to improve performance. In the cartwheel, for example, he may not be aware that his legs are bent. In such instances the teacher or coach should supply feedback information. This is termed augmented feedback, the supply of which is one of the most important functions of teachers and coaches seeking to improve pupils' skill. A distinction has been drawn between two forms of feedback, that of knowledge of results and knowledge of performance. It has been suggested that knowledge of performance is most appropriate for 'closed' skills such as gymnastic movements because knowledge of results only provides information relating to the success or failure of the movement, and not necessarily to the qualitative aspect which is extremely important in gymnastics. Knowledge of results is more appropriate for 'open' skills because the individual is primarily concerned with the consequences of his actions. For a discussion of 'open' and 'closed' skills see Knapp (1963: 150–157). In an experiment involving basketball shooting, Wallace and Hagler (1979) concluded that knowledge of performance is a strong feedback source in the acquisition of a closed motor skill.

Motivation

Gymnasts must be motivated if they are to acquire skills and perform efficiently. We will indicate only the fundamental issues related to the nature of motivation in this section since a separate chapter has been devoted to this topic. The study of motivation is an attempt to seek for causes of behaviour. All behaviour may be considered as having two dimensions, that of direction and intensity. The gymnast attending gym club and practising in order to improve his skill level is said to be demonstrating approach behaviour. A pupil who avoids gym club is said to be showing avoidance behaviour. The behaviour demonstrated, either approach or avoidance will occur at a given intensity. This dimension is referred to as arousal level. A boy running down to the gym after school, excited at the prospect of vaulting over boxes, is demonstrating a higher level of arousal than the boy who slowly walks down, not so excited at the prospect of training. When a gymnast performs a particular move he does so at a certain arousal level. Sometimes it will be the correct level for good performance, at other times it will be too high or too low. The relationship between arousal level and optimum performance has been the subject of considerable research, some of which is discussed in Chapter five.

Approaches to the study of skills acquisition

The reasons for changes in performance which occur as a person learns gymnastic skills are complex. Early approaches to the subject arose from behaviourist and cognitive (Gestalt) schools of psychology. In recent years however there has been a proliferation of approaches.

Many of these are of an interdisciplinary nature incorporating concepts from psychology, physiology, computer science and cybernetics. This section will introduce two contrasting approaches to the study of skills acquisition and will illustrate how teaching strategies may be developed from these theoretical perspectives.

BEHAVIOURISM

The behaviourist approach is to study external behaviour. It is argued that a theory of internal processes is not necessary in order to understand human behaviour. Early behaviourism claimed that consciousness was neither a definite nor a usable concept. A scientific approach was adopted which eliminated subjective terms such as perception, purpose and even thinking. The stimulus (cues) and resultant responses were the main forms of study. Avoidance of mentalistic phenomenon occasionally reached extreme proportions. Mahoney (1974: 6) reports on a conference where it was suggested that the word 'mind' was eliminated from the vocabulary. Initially this suggestion was somewhat light hearted, however it subsequently became a matter that was given some credence. Hence *remind me* became *re-cue me* and *slipped my mind* became *has left my current behavioural repertoire*. The behaviourist emphasis on overt behaviour also gave rise to the now classic joke about two friends meeting on a street. One looks at the other and says, 'You're looking well, how am I?'

Early behaviourism was very theoretical. It gave little infomation on how to train people to acquire skills. During the Second World War this knowledge was essential as many men had to be trained to use new weaponry and learn combat skills. Accordingly, a strong task orientated approach arose. Skills were classified and principles of training were established largely by adopting a trial and error approach. The behaviourist approach is still very much alive today although certain changes have occurred from the early days. Considerable emphasis has been laid, for example, on developing teaching strategies. The approach concentrates on shaping desired responses. Topics such as reaction time are considered as of academic interest, having no relevance to actual teaching and coaching. In order to shape a response such as a handspring, on emphasis is placed on carefully structuring a situation so that the required skill is made by the performer. When the correct move is made it is positively reinforced by the use of praise and rewards. Rushall and Siedentop (1972) have developed a strategy for teaching and coaching sports skills based on principles of operant psychology (a major school of thought in Behaviourism). This strategy will be discussed later in the chapter.

The behaviouristic approach has led to the development of behaviour therapy techniques for the control of emotional responses. Treatment for fears and phobias using relaxation and visualisation techniques have been very successful. These techniques are now widely used to enhance sports performance and some approaches are discussed in the chapter on motivation. In recent years behaviourists have begun to shift their stance. Concepts such as perception are becoming acceptable. Neisser (1967) remarked on the shifting emphasis of behaviourism when he stated that S — R theorists are now inventing hypothetical mechanisms with vigour and enthusiasm and only a twinge of conscience! Further evidence of this shifting emphasis comes from the field of behaviour modification. This is in itself a recent arrival on the applied clinical scene, yet an area of study called cognitive behaviour modification has already begun to emerge. As Mahoney (1974) points out there is an emerging era of the 'thinking behaviourist'. There is an acceptance that an individual responds not to some real environment but to a perceived environment.

INFORMATION PROCESSING AND COGNITIVE PSYCHOLOGY

Cognitive psychology arose as a reaction against radical behaviourism. It was the work of the Gestalt psychologists in the early part of this century which foreshadowed the development of this school of thought. There was little progress however until the last twenty five years as psychology was dominated by Behaviourism. The cognitive position emphasises the mental processes that influence behaviour. It is proposed that perception and interpretation of an event rather than the event itself often accounts for behaviour. A large noisy crowd may cause one competitor to become very nervous. The same noise may be perceived by another competitor as exciting. Subsequent performances may reflect these differing perceptions. Cognitive theories have shown an interest in the indi-

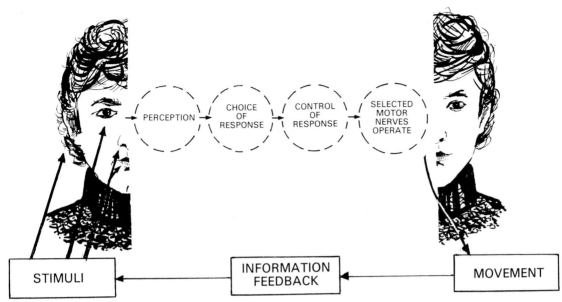

A simplified model showing the hypothetical mechanisms involved in information processing

vidual, his personality and thought processes. Events within the person are as important as environmental stimuli.

One of the main influences which accounted for the re-emergence of cognitive psychology was the development of the information processing approach. This approach grew out of the application theory, (a branch of communication science which provided an abstract way of analysing the processing of knowledge), to research on human skill and performance. An attempt is made to explain human performance by following the flow of information through the various processes. Information processing models provide a framework for examining limitations of attention perceptions, memory and decision making in the performance of skills.

Early attempts to apply information theory models to skills acquisition concentrated on measuring the amount of information a person could process. An emphasis was laid on man's capacity to attend to and register stimuli in the environment. Studies were frequently concerned with the time factor in decision making. Information theory was used to explain variations in the speed of responses (reaction time). Skilled performers usually react more quickly and more accurately. Explanations for this were based on the ability to detect and process information from the environment.

While research was being carried out on information measurement a further development was taking place. Another branch of the information sciences, that of computer programming, was applied to research into skilled performance. These two developments have evolved into the information processing approach to skilled performance. Discoveries made by information processing theorists have contributed considerably to an understanding of how variables such as psychological stress influence performance and how the internal processes operate during performance.

Computer programmes have much in common with theories of cognition. It was this aspect of information processing which was seized upon and utilised to develop the cognitive approach. The cognitive psychologist tries to give an account of the way information is processed in computer terms. While other types of analysis exist in cognitive psychology, information processing holds a dominant position. It can be seen therefore that the development of an information processing approach has had two effects. It has enabled researchers to make a coherent study of skilled performance and has initiated the *'cognitive revolution'*.

The main emphasis in cognitive psychology is on attempts to understand mental processes such as perception, memory and thinking. Particular attention was initially given to intellectual processes. It is only in the last decade that motor control has come under the scrutiny of cognitive psychologists. (Harvey, N., Greer, K. 1980). The result is that in addition to concepts based on the 'traditional' information processing approach (eg Welford 1976) there are newer concepts arising from cognitive psychology. Many of them use information terminology and computer analogies and there is often an overlap between the various approaches. Harvey and Greer review many of these approaches in an attempt to convey an emerging coherence of the cognitive psychology of action.

A number of experiments have illustrated the need for a more complex analysis of behaviour than behaviourism. Murray (1979) investigated the effect of different teaching strategies on pupils with differing cognitive styles. Individuals were tested for differences in cognitive styles and were categorised and grouped as either sequential information processors (small amounts of information related to a skill are processed sequentially) or wholistic information processors (people who prefer to try to process all the relevant information as a whole). Following this, subjects were taught to juggle. Half of each of the two groups of subjects were taught using the part-whole method. The skill was broken down into parts which were subsequently joined together to give the whole skill. The remainder of the subjects were taught to juggle using the 'whole' method. The results clearly showed that sequential learners learnt more quickly using the part method and wholistic learners learnt more quickly using the whole method.

This experiment shows that learning efficiency can be increased by implementing appropriate instructional strategies to meet the unique needs of the individual learner. Although great care must be taken in generalising to other skills it does suggest that the gymnastics coach of elite performers could improve his efficiency by ascertaining the cognitive mode of his pupils and modifying his approach to the teaching of skills accordingly. Obviously more research specifically related to gymnastic skills is required but these results seriously question the strict adherence to progressive practices for pupils and a stereotyped presentation for skill development.

The cognitive approach has led to a reappraisal of the concepts of stress and emotion. In a later chapter the influence of fear on perfor-

mance will be discussed but it is worth pointing out at this stage that environmental situations do not cause stress or emotion. It is the person's interpretation of the situation that leads to emotional responses. The teacher and coach can have a great influence on a performer's interpretation of the situation. Lindsay and Norman (1977) report on an ingenious experiment by Schacter and Singer who produced strong evidence for a cognitive theory of emotions. They showed that for people to interpret an internally aroused state as being emotional depends on the context in which the arousal occurs. In addition, when people perceive themselves as being in an emotional state, the nature of the emotion will depend again on the context in which they find themselves (see illustration below).

A behaviouristic approach to teaching skills

As mentioned earlier, in this approach a person's behaviour is the main focus of attention. This includes not only what a person does but also what he says either overtly or to himself (thinking). A verbal instruction given by a coach for example, is considered just as objective a type of behaviour as performing a handspring. Most behaviour can be seen or heard and as such is observable, measurable and capable of objective analysis. It may be necessary however to use monitoring devices in order to obtain information on certain behavioural responses. Changes in heart rate, for example, may require the use of an electrocardiograph. The behaviourist sees behaviour in terms of stimulus and response. Certain stimuli arising from the environment have the effect of eliciting a particular response. It is the study of this relationship which forms the basis of the behaviourists approach.

Fundamental to this approach is the belief that behaviour is determined by the environment. This includes everything that has an effect on the performer and includes the performer's previous behaviour. The presentation of stimuli to a gymnast can be controlled to a certain extent by the teacher or coach. Accordingly the skill of teaching and coaching lies in arranging the environment to achieve goals (terminal behaviours). He should shape responses which result in better performance. In order to achieve this it is necessary to understand something of the theories and principles of learning which have been developed as a result of the scientific analysis of behaviour in a variety of settings. Many of these principles can be directly applied

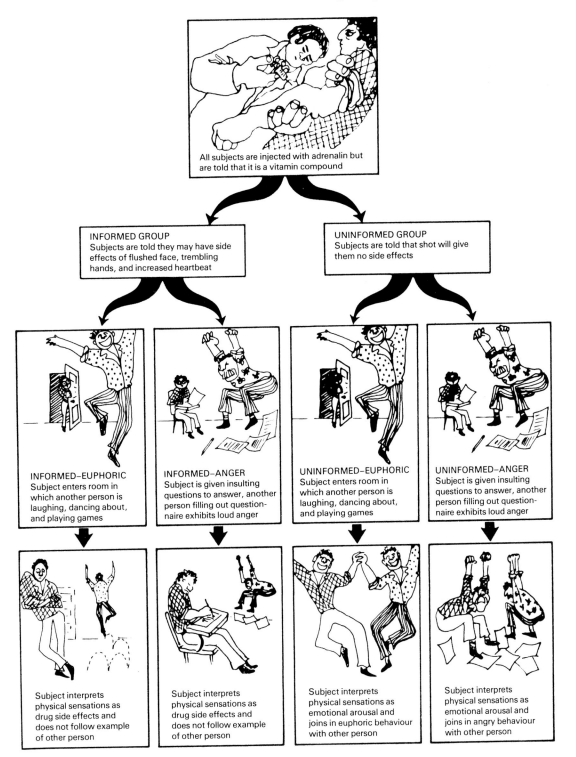

Schacter and Singer's experiment on arousal and emotion

From *Human Information Processing* by P. H. Lindsay and D. A. Norman published by Academic Press Inc Ltd, New York 1972.

to develop teaching strategies for skills acquisition. Rushall and Siedentop (1972) have provided a text which gives a practical set of principles for the development and control of behaviour in sport. The information given in this section relies heavily on their text. Unlike other motor learning texts they deal specifically with strategies arising from the school operant psychology (a dominant approach in Behaviourism). They consider topics such as reaction time, peripheral visual activity and movement time as of academic interest only. Measurable behaviour is considered as the only legitimate aspect of study. In the case of gymnastics this refers to the predominance of the various skills ivolved. The primary concern of teaching physical education and coaching sports, they claim, is the production of changes in behaviour such as helping a child to improve his round off. After this has been achieved the task of the teacher and coach is to produce stability in the behaviour so that they will remain at the desired level for a long time. This involves what is normally referred to as maintaining motivation to practice. Behaviourists, however, prefer to dispel with conjecture on internal needs and drives. Maintaining motivation is considered a question of 'contingency management'. Terms such as this have been introduced by behaviourists who have developed principles of learning based on operant psychology. It is necessary therefore to examine some of these terms before teaching strategies can be discussed.

RESPONSES AND OPERANTS

A differentiation is made between a response and an operant. The former is a single performance such as an attempt at a backward roll. The latter is a class of responses which bring about a change in a person's environment in a similar way. Backward rolling, therefore, is an operant as each attempt will bring about similar changes in the person's immediate environment. Operants are also susceptible to the same reinforcers such as the feeling of satisfaction which usually accompanies each successful attempt.

STIMULUS

A *stimulus* is a classifiable environmental event. Examples are a forehand drive in tennis, a basketball rebounding from the backboard, a verbal instruction. In gymnastics, achieving the angled, overbalanced position in the headspring

on the broad horse may be considered as a stimulus. Some stimuli are said to be *discriminative*. This is a particular stimulus which precedes and controls one or more behaviours. They indicate the time and/or situation for a specific behaviour to be made. Teaching and coaching sports skills is largely dealing with *discriminative stimuli*. It involves helping a performer recognise a particular stimulus and then conditioning the required response. If a specific response to a discriminative stimulus has been positively reinforced on a number of occasions then that stimulus will develop strong control over that response. A gymnast, for example, must recognise the *feel* of being in the angled overbalanced position. This *feel* acts as a discriminative stimulus and indicates the time for the responses of throwing the legs and pushing off the box. If he does this and successfully lands on his feet then the response will be positively reinforced. Accordingly, the overbalanced position will become a strong discriminative stimulus. Each time he achieves that position he will throw his legs and push. Verbal instructions and demonstrations are referred to as *primers*. They act as discriminative stimuli since they set a situation for an appropriate behaviour.

Some stimuli have a reinforcing effect. A reinforcer is a stimulus which occurs as an event after a performance of an operant (eg a through vault) and causes a change in the probability of that operant occurring again. The probability will be decreased if the gymnast performs badly (negative reinforcement). It is important to recognise that sitmuli can change from one category to another. A handspring to land in a crouched position may intially produce positive reinforcement but at a later stage, when the gymnast is attempting an extended landing the crouched position may produce negative reinforcement.

It is often beneficial to give consideration to the pattern of reinforcement to be given. This is referred to as the *schedule of reinforcement*. The quickest way to establish a behaviour such as a technically good performance of a through vault is to reinforce every response. This is called *continuous reinforcement*. A *ratio schedule* refers to the number of responses that must be emitted before one response is reinforced. An example in gymnastics would be asking a gymnast to give five technically sound performances of the forward roll. After the fifth attempt he can tick-off that skill on a progress chart. An *interval schedule* of reinforcement refers to the amount of time that must elapse before a response is reinforced eg a gymnast must practise achieving the splits position for five minutes before being given positive reinforcement. At a later stage he can discriminate from among the proprioceptive stimuli and make the appropriate response at the correct time without verbal instructions.

CONTINGENCY MANAGEMENT

Contingency refers to the relationship between a behavioural response and the consequences of that response. Thus 'contingencies of reinforcement' refer to the stimuli in the environment when a response is made, the response itself and the nature of the subsequent reinforcement which occurs. Behaviourists consider teaching to be a process of changing behaviour by controlling and organising the relationship between behaviour and its consequences. This is termed 'contingency management'.

Principles of contingency management provide a systematic method for shaping desired responses such as performing gymnastic skills successfully and maintaining behaviours generally. For a discussion of contingency management, see Rushall and Siedentop (1972: 175).

Teaching strategies for developing and modifying behaviour

The application of contingency management principles derived from operant psychology to teaching physical education has enabled Rushall and Siedentop to develop two models, one for teaching a new behaviour, another for changing a skill. Both models are shown below with examples from gymnastics. Rushall and Siedentop propose that the potential for changing and developing responses lies in the manipulation of the environment, arranging and ordering stimulus presentation and reinforcement. There are a number of considerations for shaping skilled performance. One of the most important is the nature of the terminal behaviour. Some skills are composed of a number of parts. Accordingly, skilled performance requires the chaining of responses. In such cases the 'macro' skill should be broken down and taught in parts. Another important consideration is the role of 'priming behaviour' (guidance). Primers act as discriminative stimuli for the gymnast as they indicate the appropriate response to be made. Behaviour which is desirable should be consistently emitted and undesir-

able behaviour should be eliminated by the correct use of positive and negative reinforcement.

A model for teaching a new behaviour

This model applies to circumstances where the terminal behaviour is not in the individual's repertoire. Circumstances such as learning to perform a handspring and to do a somersault are examples of new activities. Rushall Siedentop also point out that the development of non-skilled behaviours eg assertive behaviours, may also be carried out using this model. The steps required for an adequate shaping strategy are listed below using the neckspring on the broad horse as an example of how they apply to teaching a gymnastic skill.

1 *Determine the terminal behaviour.* (In this instance, a technically sound performance of the neckspring is the required terminal behaviour.)

2 *Determine one or more significant reinforcers.* (Ensure that performers receive knowledge of performance, knowledge of results, praise and success. Promotion to a higher ability on successfully performing a part practice, displaying a chart of skills acquired by the gymnasts and offering extrinsic rewards such as badges may all have a positive reinforcing effect.)

3 *Determine a successively more approximate set of criteria (the sequence of steps) for each behaviour or behaviour segment.* (Gradually introduce more strict performance standards eg bent legs may be allowed initially but with successive trials the need to keep the legs straight after take off should be emphasised.)

4 *For complex skills determine the appropriate sequence for teaching the segments and their amalgamation so that the skill will be built efficiently.* (The neckspring can be broken down into part practices which become successively nearer to the whole skill eg pupils initially practise forward rolls on a platform of benches – see page 16 for details of progressive practices for the neckspring.)

5 *Determine methods for administering contingent reinforcement.* (Lessons or coaching sessions should be carefully planned so that the maximum amount of knowledge of

results is given by the teacher or coach to each pupil. In addition, consideration may have to be given concerning the award of badges, house points, prizes and promotion.)

6 *Determine the reinforcement schedules and desired behaviour strengths for each step.* (Continuous praise may be given initially and then changed to a ratio schedule eg after five successful attempts at a part practice they will be allowed to progress to a more advanced part practice or to attempt the whole skill. The neckspring should be analysed and the most important aspects identified eg shoulders in the correct position on the box top. The part practice to achieve this should be emphasised.)

7 *Determine the reinforcing schedules for establishing the terminal behaviour.* (Initially provide knowledge of results, knowledge of performance and praise each time the whole skill is performed to a high standard – continuous reinforcement. This may be changed later to a ratio or interval schedule eg practice the move ten times.)

8 *Determine procedures for developing stimulus control.* (Verbal instructions and demonstrations are primers which act as discriminative stimuli. They should bring about an appropriate response. Teachers and coaches should therefore carefully consider how to explain and arrange demonstrations.)

9 *Prime the behaviour segments or the behaviour itself.* (Give instructions and demonstrations.)

10 *Reinforce each step.* (Provide the reinforcement and the schedule chosen for each part practice.)

11 *Apply the terminal schedule when the progress is completed.* (Provide the reinforcement schedule chosen when the neckspring on the broad horse is performed.)

12 *Appraise the terminal behaviour periodically and reinstitute shaping procedures and terminal schedule where necessary.* (Arrange for the neckspring to be practised in future sessions or in the group work part of subsequent lessons. Concentrate on eliminating errors which may recur.)

A MODEL FOR CHANGING A SKILL

This model applies to circumstances where the behaviour exists in some form but needs to be modified in order to improve performance. In the straddle vault, for example, the legs may be bent and too low. It differs from the previous model in the planning stages and in the singular approach to changing one feature of the skill at a time.

1 *Recognise the features of the established movement pattern which need to be replaced. This should be listed.*
2 *Determine and list the replacement patterns.*
3 *Determine one or more significant reinforcers.*
4 *Determine the steps for shaping. Since the individual will already perform a 'comfortable' technique, these steps must be gradually introduced.*
5 *Develop a programme for changing one feature at a time so that the skill is systematically rebuilt.*
6 *Determine methods for administering contingent reinforcement.*
7 *Determine step reinforcement schedules.*
8 *Determine terminal behaviour reinforcement schedules.*
9 *Let the individual know what is being done incorrectly in the skill. Motivate the performer to avoid the feature in question as the programme is followed.*
10 *Prime each feature as it is planned.*
11 *Reinforce each step.*
12 *Apply the terminal schedule.*
13 *Appraise the skill and reinstitute schedules or programme sequences where necessary.*
14 *Perform the activity in the actual or simulated environment.*

One of the most important factors in the implementation of these strategies is a teacher's knowledge and ability to implement a number of progressive practices for complex skills. In addition he must be able to identify inefficient responses and build up efficient patterns. This can only be achieved by having a good technical knowledge of the skills involved.

Reinforcement is a key issue in changing performance. The successful performance of gymnastic skills may provide sufficient positive reinforcement. However, it is frequently necessary to use extrinsic rewards such as praise and badges. One of the most significant reinforcers for shaping behaviour is knowledge of results. A number of ingenious methods have been used. A flashing light system was used to improve a swimmer's butterfly action. During each breathing phase he looked at a light at the end of the pool, the beam of which was directed at him. If the beam was off it indicated the new technique was being performed correctly. The coach switched on the beam when an error was made. This method enabled the swimmer to receive knowledge of results immediately after the completion of each stroke.

CRITICISMS OF THE BEHAVIOURIST APPROACH

Prior to Rushall and Siedentop's attempt to establish the behaviourist position there had been little interest in this approach. The human performance approach which emphasised the processing of information had attracted most attention. This was partly due to the criticisms which have been levelled at behaviourism. These cirticisms are still in evidence today. Nevertheless Rushall and Siedentop's book *The Development and Control of Behaviour in Sport and Physical Education* is refreshing in its application of theory to practice and is highly recommended for teachers and coaches of gymnastics.

At first glance the application of a behaviourist approach appears to be a logical and most suitable approach to teaching gymnastics. Teaching skills may be considered as a process of conditioning the correct behavioural responses. However, a teacher or coach should realise that reinforcement of responses is not always under his control. For example, a performer practising on his own may be successfully landing on his feet after performing a handspring. This will provide positive reinforcement but he may also be *'grooving in'* an incorrect hip action. Unless identified by the teacher and modified it could hinder progress and development of the move.

An accumulation of experimental evidence over recent years has suggested the need for a more complex analysis of behaviour than the behaviourist approach. This is particularly true in the study of skilled performance be it the competence of the manual craftsman, the car driver or the skill of the gymnast. It can be argued that the behaviourist approach does not address itself to the very details of skilled performance which make it interesting, namely the patterning of movements, the way each movement is monitored and controlled during the execution and the way one movement flows into another.

Behaviouristic theory limits itself to the assumption that behaviour is a product of acquired responses and acts which have effects on the stimulus environment. It tends to overlook the role of consciousness and refuses to speculate about intervening; processes taking place in the people that they are observing. Consequently the approach has been criticized as being too mechanistic, man being viewed as 'no more than a wind-up automatom, a bundle of conditioned reflexes and habits – totally at the mercy of its particular history of reinforced, or prevailing stimulus conditions.' (Medcof and Roth: 142).

Human performance: an information processing approach

Whereas the focus in the behaviourist approach is on the effect of a response on subsequent responses, information processing emphasises the limitations of man's ability to attend to and perceive stimuli, to develop memories and to make decisions.

> 'The capacity of the learner to handle a number of cues, to transmit information at a fast rate, to retrieve information from memory stores, is of interest to information processing theorists.'
>
> Singer (1975: 80)

In sport, the performer has to take in information from both external and/or internal sources, make a decision regarding this information and subsequently make the appropriate response. Information processing theorists seek to explain how the processes which are involved operate. The approach originated in the 50s, since then an increasing number of models of skilled behaviour have been developed. Some have concentrated on the communication aspect where the processes of coding information (perception), translation, transmission and storage of information are emphasised. Others concentrate on the control systems, paying particular attention to the role of feedback. Adaptive systems models have also been developed. These hypothesise the existence of hierarchical processes. They have been developed by comparing computer operations to brain functioning. Skills are considered as being produced through the exist-

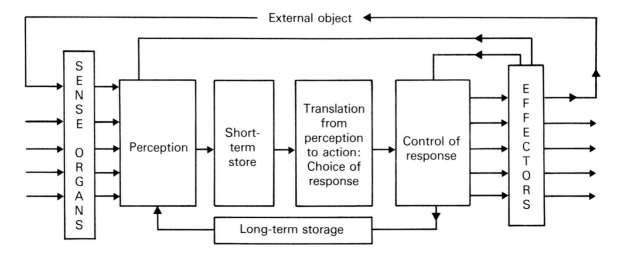

Hypothetical block diagram of the human sensorimotor system. Only a few of the many feedback-loops which exist are shown. (From A. T. Welford, Fundamentals of Skill, Methuen, London 1968)

ence of higher order (executive) programmes or routines and subroutines. Executive programmes can be thought of as a plan or idea. Accordingly, running to the mat and performing a round off flic flac may be considered as an executive programme. Reaching for the mat with both hands, swinging one leg up, half turning to bring both legs down together are examples of possible subroutines in the executive plan. Subroutines may be considered as foundational building blocks which contribute, in sequential order to performance of a skill. At early learning stages the higher order executive routines function with higher order subroutines. The performer must attend to information about the various 'parts' in order to perform successfully. At a later stage these higher order routines 'delegate' their authority to lower order routines. This frees the system to attend to other information. The hierarchical concept of control over movement helps to explain why well learned gymnastic skills can be performed almost automatically.

One of the most influential models to stimulate and guide further research was that devised by Welford (1968). He proposed an information processing system with limited channel capacity.

In his book *Skilled Performance: Perceptual and Motor Skills* Welford (1976) takes the view that the basis of skilled performance is the efficient and effective use of capacities as the result of experience and practice. He suggests that the chain of central mechanisms leading

from sensory input to motor output fall into three main divisions:
(i) perceptual coding,
(ii) choice of response (translation from perception to response),
(iii) the phasing and sequencing of action.

All these stages, he says, are concerned with more or less complex computations based upon incoming information, but also incorporating influences from the previous state of the organism stored in short and long term memory systems. Feedback loops within the individual together with knowledge of results of his actions make the whole system a self regulating servomechanism. Some of the mechanisms involved in the central chain proposed by Welford are discussed below since the concepts involved have implications for teaching and coaching sports skills.

PERCEPTUAL CODING

Perceptual processes are responsible for making sense of the information received. Both selection and integration of incoming data is involved. A vast amount of information is available at any one time, far more than the individual can attend to. Accordingly he selectively attends to only part of the information. The process involved may be compared to a filter which is biased for or against certain information in the display. Bias towards attending to or ignoring certain information results from such factors as familiarity, expectations and aims. There is a certain amount of truth in the saying *'we see what we want to see'.*

Information received from the various external and internal sources must be integrated into a pattern. This may be done by the application of an internal pattern or 'schemata' to the information registered. As a result of numerous experiences we build schemata. They are important knowledge structures that help us to deal effectively with the information processing demands placed on us by a vast amount of information being available. They help us to recognise objects, make judgements and perform skills. An expert gymnastics judge, for example, will have built up schemata of, for example, a perfect flic-flac or a perfect back somersault. The application of this schemata to the performance he is judging will cause him to note deviations from the perfect move.

The application of 'schemata' to information registered can however cause problems. It appears that they tend to shape perception by adding to the percept details in the familiar schemata which were not actually there. In addition, details in the data available may be ignored if they do not fit the schemata. Thus while the application of schemata helps us to deal with a lot of information they have been described as *'quick and dirty'* methods of thinking (Anderson, J. R. 1980: 158). In an article on errors of judgement Low (1978) suggested that the neglect of data actually present but not in the imposed schemata may lead to performance errors. The formation of schemata has received considerable attention from cognitive psychologists in recent years. Implications for teaching gymnastic skills are discussed later.

CHOICE OF RESPONSE

During the execution of a floor exercise the expert gymnast receives a continual flow of information. This information forms the basis of subsequent responses as he attempts to maintain a high level of skill. It may be necessary on occasions to make a choice of response. He may for example, register information that he has performed a round off badly. He must then choose his next response, either to try to adjust and continue with the next move as planned or change to an alternative response. Performance of a floor exercise is a good example of continuous decision making. Information must be computed

in a fraction of a second and appropriate decisions made.

EFFECTOR MECHANISMS

These mechanisms are responsible for producing motor action. Appropriate muscle groups are selected to perform a particular act. In addition, their sequential ordering of firing must be arranged and timed correctly if the desired skill is to be performed successfully. The information which a gymnast or coach perceives leads to a decision being made concerning the choice of response. Decisions are relayed to the effectors via the translation mechanisms. The orders which the effectors receive may be incorrect resulting in the wrong muscle groups being made to function. This will result in inappropriate actions being initiated. Adjustments then become necessary if the intended outcome is still to be achieved. In the cartwheel, for example, the experienced gymnast will be constantly adjusting his muscular responses according to the information received concerning his speed, balance and position.

The detection of errors in the selection of muscle groups may occur as a result of feedback from a response. It has been proposed (Adams 1971; Schmidt 1975) that feedback information results in the formation of a *perceptual trace* or *recognition schema*. In the cartwheel for instance, feedback from a number of trials (which eventually lead to success at acquiring the skill) result in the formation of a perceptual trace or recognition schema of the correct movement pattern. This trace acts as a reference mechanism. In successive attempts at the cartwheel the feedback produced allows the responses made to be compared to the existing perceptual trace or recognition schema resulting in error detection and correction of performance during its execution.

THE EFFECT OF STRESS AND AROUSAL ON INFORMATION PROCESSING

When a gymnast performs a particular skill he does so at a certain level of intensity. He may be performing in a smooth relaxed manner, alternatively, he may be performing with a high degree of effort and tension. This intensity dimension of behaviour is referred to as *arousal level*. It is generally accepted that there is an optimum level of arousal for the performance of a skill. In information processing terms this indicates that there is an optimum level which must be attained if the maximum amount of information is to be processed. In general terms a moderate level of arousal allows the greatest amount of information to be utilised. Below this level the performer may be too inattentive and fail to detect information such as loss of balance until it is too late to make the necessary adjustments. Above the optimum, ie at a high arousal level, the performer may be considered as being under stress. This may arise from psychological and/or physical factors. It is important that teachers and coaches remember that individuals have a limited capacity for processing information and that this capacity is reduced under conditions of high arousal. It is pointless, therefore, to try to give numerous coaching points to a performer who is obviously anxious about attempting a difficult move.

The optimum level of arousal varies according to the nature of the task and the level of the skill of the performer. An expert may not need to process as much information as a novice. In a cartwheel into handspring, for example, the expert will probably only be attending to information related to the achievement of good lift and flight. The novice must attend to many other factors such as hand position, balance and body position after the cartwheel. Since the expert needs to attend to less information for successful performance he can therefore tolerate a higher level of arousal. He often, in fact, needs a high level of arousal for good performance if he is to produce for example, a move with good flight. Certain gymnastic skills require more information to be processed than others. Some sequences within the floor exercise may require the performer to monitor a considerable amount of information as there may be a change of pace and level involved, in addition to the execution of specific responses.

Application of information processing to the teaching of gymnastic skills

Teachers and coaches of gymnastic skills can benefit considerably by considering some of the basic concepts involved in the information processing approach. Of particular importance is the role of schemata formation in skills acquisition. The performer, whether child or adult, often comes to the learning situation with a large amount of past experience relevant to

the performance of the new skill. The teacher, therefore should structure his presentation to allow for the pupil to selectively attend initially to the similarities. Subsequent trials will allow him to build up a schema of the new move. When teaching the one-handed cartwheel, for example, the performer may be asked initially to cartwheel normally but think about not taking any weight on the first hand. With successive trials less and less weight can be placed on this hand as his schemata of the 'feel' of a cartwheel is modified to produce a new schemata of the one-handed cartwheel. Skill is specific, accordingly practice sessions should allow for the development of specific schemata. It has been proposed that learning is a process of modifying the initial schemata formed as a result of the first attempt to perform the skill. This modification occurs through feedback arising from subsequent attempts. If this is the case then teachers must make every effort to ensure that the first attempts are as near as possible to the correct action.

When teaching a complicated gymnastic skill the teacher is faced with a decision of either teaching the skill as a whole or breaking it down into parts. The most appropriate method depends on the nature of the skill and possibly the learning style of the pupil. In order to perform a complex skill the learner must pay attention to a considerable amount of information in order to be successful. Often it is not possible to attend to all the relevant information. Accordingly, he may suffer from 'information overload' and produce a bad performance as he has failed to respond to some vital cues. It is often better therefore to break complex skills down into parts. Thus the learner is presented with only the amount of information he can handle.

Part-whole teaching may be related to the computer analogy discussed earlier. The parts may be considered sub-routines which are later combined and the whole programme is practised. Although part-whole teaching is widely used and have achieved good results considerable thought should be given to the nature of the skill before breaking it down into parts. If good performance of a skill relies on a smooth flow of responses, such as in the cartwheel, it may be unwise to teach the move in parts. Care must be taken to ensure that the part practiced is performed in such a way as to ensure that positive transfer occurs when it is linked to another part. Practising the take-off for a standing back somersault by jumping and tucking the knees is often ineffective because unless strong support is given, the take-off position differs from that required for the actual somersault.

The information processing approach places considerable emphasis on the role of feedback. A performer generally has knowledge of results but the teacher should augment this by providing knowledge of performance. How the skill is performed, not just whether the performer regained his feet or not, is of particular importance in the execution of the gymnastic skills.

Summary

There are many approaches to the study of skills acquisition. In order to show the disparity between approaches, two contrasting views have been discussed and applied to the acquisition of gymnastic skills. The behaviourist approach emphasises the study of overt behaviour. It is argued that a theory of internal processes is not necessary in order to understand human behaviour. The approach is based on the belief that responses are made as a result of receiving certain stimuli. Gymnastic skills then can be developed by arranging the appropriate stimulus conditions. The responses which are subsequently made can be shaped by carefully structuring the situation so that the required skill is made by the performer. Thus the skill of teaching and coaching lies in arranging the environment to achieve goals. Extensive use is made of praise and reward (positive reinforcement).

Early learning theories based on the behaviourist approach were of little value in the development of teaching strategies. In recent years however, strategies have been developed which are based on principles of operant psychology. These strategies are based on a structured approach to shaping desired responses by determining goals and providing effective forms of reinforcement. Considerable success has been attained by coaches who have utilised these strategies.

The behaviourist approach has led to the development of behaviour therapy techniques for the control of emotional responses. Treatment of fears and phobias using relaxation and visualisation techniques have been very successful. These techniques are now frequently used in the psychological preparation of superior sportsmen and women for high level competition.

The development of an information process-

ing approach arose as researchers sought for more knowledge of brain functioning in human performance. Information processing models provide a framework for examining limitations of attention, perceptions, memory and decision making in the performance of skills. Information received from the various external and internal sources must be integrated into a pattern. This is possibly carried out by the application of an internal pattern of schemata to the information registered. As a result of numerous experiences we build schemata. They are important knowledge structures which help us to perform and recognise skills.

Teachers and coaches may teach more effectively if they are aware of some of the basic concepts involved in information processing theory. Schemata formation, information overload and feedback are examples of important considerations when teaching gymnastic skills.

The information processing approach, together with developments in computer technology, was largely responsible for the re-emergence of cognitive psychology. In the last decade cognitive psychologists have turned their attention to skilled motor performance. Some of the discoveries made by cognitive psychologists, for example, differing learning styles and a cognitive approach to the study of emotional responses have important implications for the successful teaching of gymnastic skills.

CHAPTER FIVE

Motivation, emotion and fear in gymnastics

The study of motivation is an attempt to seek for causes of behaviour and to understand why people behave as they do. Needs, wants, wishes and desires are all words that one uses to explain why people carry out a particular act. In order to understand why a person is motivated to learn gymnastic skills his underlying needs must be examined. Some of these such as the need for activity and stimulation are comparatively simple to understand. However, these needs can be satisfied by any physical activity. Why is gymnastics chosen or why is soccer chosen? It can be seen therefore that the choice of behaviour is the primary motivational question. Why does one boy continue to practise the handspring while another avoids the situation? A closer examination of this question reveals the complexity of motivated behaviour which is often the result of the interaction of many motives and emotions such as achievement, excitement and fear.

The hedonistic approach to motivation contends that human beings approach goals or engage in activities which will bring pleasure. Activities which are expected to have unpleasant or aversive outcomes are avoided. The model shown on page 105 and discussed below is based on this approach. The starting point in studying motivated behaviour, as shown in the model is an examination of the antecedent conditions. What stimulus initiates the action? If a pupil attempts a handspring it may be as a result of a verbal instruction from the teacher or coach. Alternatively it may be the result of an internal desire to acquire the skill.

Often people do not just react mechanically to a stimulus. There is a mediating process which takes place within the person. He may, for example, consider the outcome of attempting a handspring and if he decides it will bring pain rather than pleasure he may avoid practising the

skill. The cognitive processes involved may also lead him to consider the value of practising the handspring. If it is seen as a valuable activity then he is likely to practise enthusiastically. Both expectancy of outcome and the value attached to acquiring a particular skill may be influenced by the teacher. He can instill confidence and help develop a positive attitude towards acquiring gymnastic skills.

Motivated behaviour may be considered to have two aspects – *direction* and *intensity*. In the former we can examine what a person is doing when reacting positively to a stimulus. This could be, for example, attempting a neckspring when asked, and in this situation the pupil may be said to be demonstrating approach behaviour. When a pupil reacts negatively to a stimulus, in this case not attempting the neckspring when asked, he may be demonstrating avoidance behaviour. The basis of refusal may well be through fear of injury. Frequently people find themselves in a conflict situation possessing a drive to approach yet at the same time to avoid a particular situation. A pupil attempting a difficult vault often stops and starts a few times at the beginning of his run up. In this case, it can be considered that the drive to practise the vault and start the run up is being interrupted by a drive to avoid the situation. If he attempts the vault, then his drive to show approach behaviour has overcome his drive for avoidance behaviour.

The other dimension of behaviour is the intensity level of motivation. This is referred to as *arousal level* and can be influenced by many factors such as determination, fear and excitement. Generally an increase in arousal leads to greater muscular tension. This may or may not be desirable, much depends on the skill being performed and the ability level and the personality of the performer. Consequently, the relationship between arousal and performance in

A model of motivated behaviour

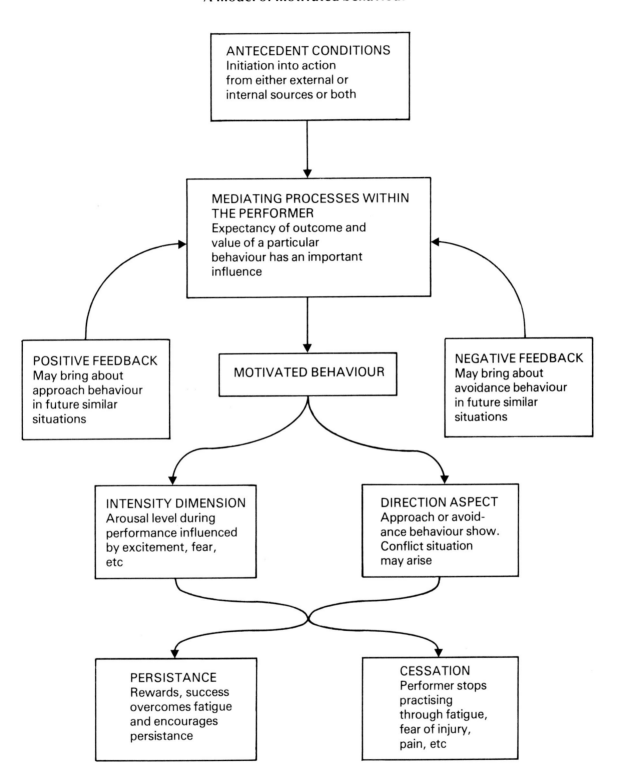

sport has received considerable attention from sport psychologists.

Once a person commences an activity, the body begins to react in order to bring that activity to a halt. Every activity eventually ceases but the length of time a person persists in practising is an important motivational consideration. Rewards and success leading to a feeling of pleasure can offset fatigue and help a person overcome fear of injury by attempting new and difficult moves.

The model which has been described above may be applied to study a specific behaviour or to take a long term view of motivation. Much of the explanation given above cites specific examples. From a long term viewpoint the mediating processes would include previous experiences and memories of similar occasions in the past. A boy may, for example, keep coming to gym club because of the enjoyment experienced by gaining skills during previous weeks. The general pattern of behaviour would be one of approach behaviour and persistence.

Sources of motivation and approach behaviour

In order to teach physical education successfully, the teacher should consider the sources of motivation. Why, for example, do children usually come running to physical education lessons? Why do they want to become more skilful? With this knowledge the teacher or coach can develop motivational techniques which he can apply to maintain his pupils' interest. Children come to physical education lessons with internal needs for activity, stimulation, competence, excitement and achievement. It is the responsibility of a teacher to manage the situation in such a way that these needs are satisfied at least in part. This will result in pupils deriving a feeling of success and pleasure from their lessons and training. It is important to realise that children should experience as many success situations as possible and as few failure situations as possible. Accordingly, the skills being taught should be carefully selected to suit the ability of the children.

The approach taken in this chapter in order to study motivation in gymnastics is to consider motivational concepts as intervening variables between antecedent conditions and consequent conditions.

Antecedent conditions	Intervening variable	Consequent conditions
Presence of audience at a gymnastics competition.	Higher neural activity (increased in arousal level).	Impaired performance of complex unlearned skills.

When the intervening variable, whether it be increased arousal or the need to acquire a specific skill, or the need for excitement, leads to a change in preference, persistence or vigour of behaviour, the intervening variable is said to be motivational.

When a person participates in gymnastics there are usually a number of variables which interact to produce this approach behaviour. In order to understand this directional aspect of motivation more fully, it is necessary to examine some of the needs which a person seeks to satisfy through participation. The interaction of these needs often results in people developing a drive to acquire sports skills. If the drive is to remain at a high level, not only must children be successful but they must also perceive that they are being successful. In traditional gymnastics, specific goals should be set by a teacher or by a child himself. It is important that children are made aware of when they have achieved success and acquired a specific skill. It should also be remembered that unsuccessful movements such as not regaining the feet in the headspring also has a positive function in learning traditional gymnastics skills. Since a specific movement pattern is being attempted, movements which fail to achieve the aim cause the gymnast to modify future attempts.

A consideration of children's needs and attitudes can help a teacher determine goals and develop teaching strategies which will bring about steady improvement. Some of the more important needs are briefly discussed below. The list is not complete but hopefully will be of assistance to teachers and coaches of gymnastics.

THE NEED FOR STIMULATION AND ACTIVITY

The need for activity may be considered as a primary drive. Healthy children are so full of energy that they cannot sit still or be quiet for long. In addition they like to test themselves to see how far they can go physically. Accordingly all physical education lessons should aim to satisfy this need. Lessons should start with an active warm up and present a physical challenge. Lengthy verbal instructions should be avoided as children want to be active. The teacher who continually interrupts children practising tends to reduce their motivation. The importance of activity has been clearly shown in experiments where exercise has been used as a form of reward (Kagan and Berkun, 1954; Hill, 1956). A continuance of a quiet state is annoying to the healthy child so he seeks activity. Closely allied to a need for activity is a need for stimulation. This leads to exploratory behaviour and play. The development of children proceeds normally only if they have sufficient stimulation. It appears that the need for stimulation has its own biological and psychological basis (Hilgard, Atkinson and Atkinson 1971: 306).

THE NEED FOR ACHIEVEMENT

The need to overcome obstacles and strive to do something difficult as well and as quickly as possible, has long been recognised as a major source of motivation. Pupils will work hard in order to gain a sense of achievement through acquiring specific gymnastics skills, providing they consider that the skill is attainable by them. Here a teacher or coach has a very important role to play. He must ensure that the skills presented are at a suitable level of difficulty and help the pupils practise with a positive attitude towards acquiring these skills. Assisting pupils to acquire skills that have a set criteria for success can satisfy this need for achievement and so develop a positive attitude towards further participation.

In a discussion on motivation Beck (1978: 318) referred to McClelland who offered a hedonic interpretation of the need for achievement. He proposed that cues previously associated with hedonically positive outcomes produced a partial rearousal of the positive effect originally experienced. Thus the individual partly experiences as well as anticipates a pleasurable outcome. In other words, if a person has been successful and obtained pleasure from a particular situation, when he finds himself in a similar situation he expects success and pleasure to result. In addition, he would be more likely to engage in further similar achievement situations. Conversely, if a person were punished for failing, a fear of failure could develop and there would be a motive to avoid similar situations. Applying this to gymnastics, it follows that children who

have enjoyed success in gymnastics lessons are more likely to show a positive attitude to further practice in subsequent lessons. This accounts for the fact that they will often happily repeat skills long after they have been acquired to a reasonable level. Children find the repetition of learned gymnastic skills pleasurable and this should be allowed for in lesson planning. It is desirable, not only for motivational reasons, but also in order to retain these skills.

Research evidence has provided strong support that behaviour is controlled by its consequences (Bandura 1973). Success and failure have a strong influence upon subsequent goal setting and how much will be achieved. A boy who continually fails to land on his feet after many attempts at a handspring soon loses interest. He must receive some success. A teacher can help him to do this by a variety of methods. He can provide physical support, encouragement, increase the child's determination to succeed or break the skill down into parts where the acquisition of successive part practices bring their own reward. A child who has experienced nothing but failure on skills taught to him will clearly have a low level of aspiration when subsequent skills are introduced. A teacher must set realistic progressive goals to each individual which lead to small but repetitive success so that success begets success. The success experienced will lead to raised aspirations. The writer has personal experience of coaching a student who for many weeks was unable to jump into a crouched position onto the horse, even with the use of a springboard. In order to help the student acquire the skill, marks were chalked on to the side of the box at varying heights, the aim was to touch a higher mark with both feet with successive practices. Success at touching the lower marks rapidly brought success at touching the higher marks. Very few trials were necessary to achieve the crouch position. Various vaulting skills were rapidly acquired once this skill had been achieved.

The satisfaction of the need for achievement by learning specific gymnastic skills can help develop a positive attitude to participation. However, there are problems associated with considering the need for achievement as a single variable. Jackson, Ahmed and Heapy (1976) postulated six distinct dimensions for achievement motivation.

1 Status with experts
2 Acquisitiveness
3 Achievement via independence
4 Status with peers
5 Competitiveness
6 Concern for excellence.

The complexity of motivation is made apparent when one realises that a person may have high achievement need for excellence but not for status with peers. This may result in him working hard to acquire a number of difficult gymnastic skills and to perform them to a high standard technically. However, he may not be highly motivated to participate in competitions or to represent this club in order to achieve status.

THE NEED TO DEVELOP SKILL

In a discussion of the concept of competence as a major motivating force, White (1959) referred to the work of Hendrick who claimed that humans have an inborn drive 'to do and learn how to do'. The aim of this drive is to achieve pleasure in exercising a function successfully. White also referred to Mittleman who came to a similar conclusion, stating that skilled motor action is an urge in its own right. The good gymnastics teacher is one who ensures that each child in his class regularly experiences the feeling of pleasure associated with fulfilling the need to acquire skill. In a paper on motivation, White (1959) considered various drives for example activity, exploration, mastery, and concluded that humans have a basic drive for competence.

THE NEED FOR EXCITEMENT

Many of our activities provide clear evidence of a need for excitement. People climb mountains or drive fast cars in order to raise their level of stimulation. Fear is often deliberately courted and it appears that such actions are inherently rewarding. Berlyne (1960) suggested that people often like experiences, eg, riding on a big dipper, which increase their arousal. He coined the phrase 'arousal jags' and points out that many things we do involve arousal jags. The presentation of challenging gymnastic skills can help satisfy the need for excitement. The gymnast frequently experiences mild forms of fear as he attempts a move which he is still learning. Controlling this fear and successfully performing the skill can be very rewarding. Accordingly, the teacher should ensure that the skills he is teaching are sufficiently challenging for the children.

The fulfillment of the needs discussed above are major goals which children seek. They are not necessarily independent but interact to produce the motivation to act in a particular way. Many needs can be satisfied through gymnastics and the teacher should carefully plan his lessons with this in mind. If he is successful, motivation to participate usually remains high.

Expectancy and value

In an earlier chapter, differing approaches to explaining the skill learning process were examined. The behaviourist approach which emphasises the relationship between a stimulus and a particular response was compared to a cognitive approach which examines how a person utilises information from the environment. How he interprets a set of stimuli and which information he attends to is considered to be very important. These differing approaches are also evident in a study on motivation. Perhaps the oldest and most central controversy in motivation is whether motivated behaviour should be conceptualised as *mechanistic* or *cognitive*. These two theoretical approaches differ in the extent to which higher mental processes are inferred and employed to account for the initiation, direction and persistence of behaviour. The current trend is towards a more cognitive approach (Weiner, B. 1972). It is argued, for example, that children develop expectancies. When asked to attempt a handspring, for example, a child may refuse as he expects to fall and hurt himself. The teacher, who is confident that the child has the ability, may be able to change his mind and encourage him to make an attempt confident that he will land safely on his feet. Remarkable progress can be achieved if the teacher can raise the children's level of aspiration and impart a feeling of confidence through positive encouragement. The cognitive approach also emphasises the role of the values which a person develops. A child who sees no value in acquiring gymnastic skills will often be working with a low level of motivation. A recent experiment (Brame 1979) showed that subjects who performed a motor task with high expectancy of success performed significantly better than subjects who performed the task with a lower expectancy of success. This has important implications for the teacher as he can influence performers' expectancies.

Expectancy x value theories stress the evaluation process that takes place in the brain as the individual subconsciously assesses the relative attractiveness of an activity as an outlet of his or her needs. Motivation is conceived as a function of internal status (motives) and situational factors (expectancy of outcome and reward value to the individual).

An interesting viewpoint on motivation has been developed by Alderman (1976). He has developed the concept of *'incentive motivation'* in sport in order to discover what it is about the sport itself that is motivating. Incentive motivation refers to the incentive value that participants attach to the possible outcomes available to him. If they feel that participation will be pleasant, enjoyable and satisfying, then they will take part. If their expectancies are confirmed from actual experiences, then they will persist in that sport and their level of motivation will remain high. If, however, expectancies are not confirmed, then interest will fall.

Research on incentive motivation has concentrated on identifying the kinds of experiences or goals that sport can provide. Goal directed behaviour appears to arise from motive-incentive systems. The major incentive systems in sport have been identified as affiliation, success, excellence, aggression, stress (seeking excitement), power and independence. Sufficient data has been gathered to suggest that the two strongest incentive conditions for young people in sport are affiliation and excellence and thirdly that of seeking excitement.

Extrinsic and intrinsic motivation

The terms 'intrinsic' and 'extrinsic' are important concepts in motivation. Deci (1975) defined intrinsic factors as those mediated by the person himself. Extrinsic factors however, are mediated by someone or something other than the athlete, such as the coach, his parents, or awards such as medals and badges. Accordingly, the gymnast who is intrinsically motivated to participate does so because he finds participation rewarding. Alternatively, a gymnast is extrinsically motivated to participate if he does so in order to achieve some external reward. Children often appear to be intrinsically motivated to learn skills. However, lack of success and fear of failure may result in their motivation being virtually non-existant. Having experienced success, children will participate for the pure enjoyment

and satisfaction of the activity itself. If, however, children are participating for other rewards, then they are extrinsically motivated. In a discussion of extrinsic and intrinsic motivation, Straub (1978: 54) suggested that when the 'pure' play of childhood is socialised into the more formal, rigid and institutionalized sport he comes under the control of extrinsic reinforcers. In gymnastics the influence of extrinsic rewards has had a marked effect on children's interest in the sport. The BAGA awards have been phenomenally successful. Children work hard to gain badges which are awarded for varying levels of proficiency.

However, there is a danger in relying too heavily on extrinsic rewards. Eventually rewards will no longer be attainable. It is possible that the proliferation of extrinsic rewards such as badges, prizes and social prestige may have a more complex effect on motivation than simply encouraging approach behaviour. It may be that they cause intrinsic motivation to be replaced by extrinsic motivation. However, the line of demarcation between intrinsic and extrinsic motivation is far from clear, indeed it is likely that there is an interaction of both forms. It has been suggested (Massimo 1976) that coaches should use extrinsic rewards on the grounds that not all learning situations eg conditioning and stretching, are such that the gymnasts would choose them of their own accord. He also advocated the use of extrinsic motivation to keep the gymnast training until intrinsic motivation takes over. This helps the gymnast through difficult periods of frustration arising from numerous unsuccessful attempts at learning a complex skill.

Avoidance behaviour and conflict

The discussion so far has been primarily concerned with approach behaviour, that is, why people are motivated to take part in sport and gymnastics in particular. How the teacher can develop and maintain this motivation has also been considered. However, in physical education lessons, some children may be demonstrating avoidance behaviour. This is the case when they are participating through fear of reprimand if they did not attend. Often this situation arises through a lack of success and pleasure during previous lessons. However, avoidance behaviour may also occur at specific times with boys who generally show approach behaviour, ie are usually keen to participate. This happens when, for example, they refuse to attempt a particular skill through fear of injury. A boy can often be seen hesitating to attempt a particular move, he is caught between two incompatible response tendencies. On the one hand he is motivated by a drive to acquire the skill, on the other hand fear of injury is motivating him to avoid the situation. It may be considered that virtually all behaviour involves conflict as there are always choices. The strength of approach or avoidance is a function of both learning and motivation. Boys will not practice well learned skills without motivation, however, strong motivation to acquire a difficult skill can overcome fear and lead to a determined attempt. The teacher can have a considerable influence on a child's response when he is in a conflict situation. Attempts should be made to reduce the fear. If he is successful the child will demonstrate approach behaviour by making an attempt at a skill. Techniques which may be used are discussed below since the concepts involved relate to the intensity dimension of motivation rather than the directional component under discussion at present.

Arousal

When the gymnast attempts a new move which he perceives as dangerous, he often exhibits a certain degree of fear. The ensuing physiological changes which occur may result in the gymnast becoming over-aroused may cause his performance to be inhibited. Gray (1971) states that fear is preferably regarded as a state not of the mind but of the neuro-endocrine system. Fear, he says, can be treated as a hypothetical state of the brain or neuro-endocrine system arising under certain conditions and eventuating in certain forms of behaviour. The frightened animal is most likely to try out one of three 'f's, *freezing*, *flight* or *fight*. These forms of behaviour are often demonstrated by novice gymnasts. They may 'freeze' on losing control half way through a vault (study a beginner making an unsuccessful attempt at a handspring on the broad horse). *'Flight'* is demonstrated when they refuse to attempt a vault and walk away from the situation. The *'fight'* reaction may be occuring when the gymnast takes a deep breath and attacks the box in determined effort to overcome his fear and make a successful vault.

This, of course, is the extreme situation. Lesser degrees of fear still cause an increase in the level of arousal. How this occurs and the relationship between arousal level and sports performance has received considerable attention. Duffy (1957) refers to arousal as a degree of excitation or energy mobilisation. She considers that behaviour varies on only two dimensions, direction and intensity. The direction of behaviour may be described as either moving toward or away from a stimulus situation, ie approach or avoidance behaviour. The person's behaviour, whether approach or avoidance, will occur at a given intensity. Accordingly, arousal may be referred to as the intensity dimension of behaviour.

This does not necessarily mean that the greater the intensity the greater will be the observable response in a given direction. The gymnast about to attempt a difficult vault, for example, may be highly aroused through fear of injury, but because he is in conflict over which way to move, ie approach and complete the vault, or avoid by refusing to attempt it, movement may be very hesitant.

In order to explain the concept of arousal and its relationship to behaviour, Martens (1974) made an analogy between human behaviour and the behaviour of an automobile. He states that one dimension of the automobile's behaviour is the speed which the engine runs, it may idle very slowly or run very fast. The intensity of the human engine is described in terms of a person's arousal level. The former can be measured with considerable accuracy, unfortunately the latter cannot. The intensity of the engine, however, tells us only in part how the car is behaving. Until it is known whether the car is in gear and whether it is in forward or reverse gear, the automobile's behaviour cannot be adequately described. Like an automobile, a gymnast's engine may be running very fast. He may, for example, be experiencing high arousal as a result of the presence of a large audience. However, he may be in 'neutral gear' as he stands waiting for the right moment to commence his floor exercise. Fear arousal is not of course the only form of arousal which gymnasts experience. Excitement at completing the first half of the floor excercise better than ever before, or a sudden gathering of determination for an explosive take off for a standing back somersault are also examples of when the gymnast may be working under a high level of arousal.

Despite the problems associated with measuring arousal level and assessing the accompanying emotion, techniques have been developed by teachers and coaches to regulate performers' arousal level for optimum performance. There can be no doubt that these techniques have caused a considerable improvement in performance in a variety of sports. Some of the methods used are discussed below. In order to gain greater insight into how these techniques operate, it is necessary to examine the relationship between arousal level and sports performance.

THE AROUSAL-PERFORMANCE RELATIONSHIP

When a gymnast stops resting and commences to perform a movement, his arousal level will increase. This increase may occur for a variety of reasons. When he concentrates on what he has to do there will be a certain amount of cortical arousal. There may also be some excitement and if an audience is present this can have an arousing effect. This increased arousal has the potential for facilitating performance on some moves while at the same time inhibiting performance on other tasks. The effect that it has is dependent on the skill and the individual characteristics of the performer. However, in general terms it can be stated that:

1 Low levels of arousal will result in slow inappropriate responses lacking in sufficient muscular tension.
2 Moderate levels of arousal have an organising effect on behaviour.
3 Under high levels of arousal, the system may be disrupted causing a lack of coordination and poor performance.

Two hypotheses have been proposed to explain the relationship between arousal and motor performance.

1 Drive theory
2 The inverted 'U' hypothesis.

DRIVE THEORY

When the gymnast performs a particular movement such as a handspring which he has perfected through numerous trials, it may be considered that he has developed a set of habitual responses which are technically correct. The level of performance, however, can still be altered by the amount of drive present (for the purpose of this discussion, drive may be equated to arousal) during the execution of the move-

ment. A low level of drive may result in a handspring lacking thrust and lift, therefore causing a relatively poor performance. If the performer has a higher drive it may result in more flight and a better movement. If this were to happen, drive theorists would argue that this supports their basic premise, *viz*:

Performance = habit x drive.

Habit refers to the hierarchial order or dominance of correct and incorrect responses. In a well learned move correct responses are dominant. When a person is in the early stages of learning, he tends to produce more incorrect responses than correct responses. In the handspring for example, the shoulders travel forward and the fully stretched position is not attained. As the skill is mastered so the correct responses become more dominant, the hands reach forward and a good body position is reached each time. An increase in drive will usually cause the dominant response to be made. In the novice this is often an incorrect set of responses, consequently increase in drive results in an increase in errors. Accordingly, the skill often breaks down completely. The expert, whose dominant responses are correct ones, can withstand a considerable increase in drive without his performance deteriorating. In fact, well-learned responses such as the thrust for lift in the handspring, may be made with more speed and power resulting in a better performance.

It follows that during the early stages of learning a skill, drive or arousal level should be kept relatively low. Situations which are likely to increase arousal such as the presence of audience and competition should be avoided. If the move elicits an increase in arousal in the performer through fear of injury, then the teacher or coach must use techniques such as those discussed below to reduce this fear. On the other hand, with the expert performer, attempts may be made to increase his arousal in order to elicit a better performance. Many coaches would agree that the height of the somersault is in direct proportion to the size of the crowd.

INVERTED 'U' HYPOTHESIS AND MOTOR PERFORMANCE

The inverted 'U' hypothesis is based on the belief that there is an optimum level of arousal for optimum performance. Performance will increase with low levels of arousal but only up

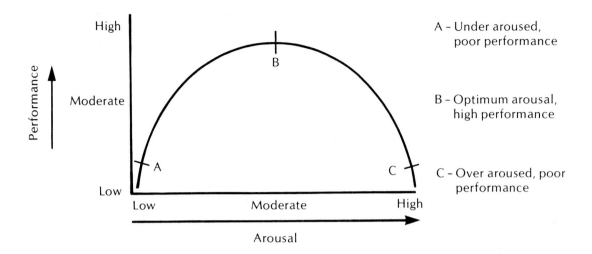

A – Under aroused, poor performance

B – Optimum arousal, high performance

C – Over aroused, poor performance

to a point after which performance will deteriorate.

The optimum level of arousal however varies according to the nature of the skill and with factors related to the individual. Tasks vary in the degree of physiological energy required and the amount of information a person must process. A running front somersault for example, requires a sudden burst of energy but apart from concentrating on a powerful take off and a tight tuck, the skilled performer has to attend to a relatively small amount of information. On the other hand, a forward roll to one leg followed by a cartwheel into handstand usually requires constant attention to technique and balance. A high degree of arousal is not necessary and may in fact impair performance through too much muscular tension. In addition, high arousal with its subsequent reduction in channel capacity may cause the gymnast to be unable to process the flow of information necessary to maintain balance and coordination.

Both the theories outlined above have been subjected to close scrutiny. In a review of research evidence, Martens (1974) concluded that the drive theory should be rejected. However, more recently Landers (1980) has pointed out that the grounds on which Martens based his conclusions were not valid. The controversy still exists today. No doubt research will eventually solve the problem but in the meantime coaches can gain a greater understanding of successful motivational techniques by studying both theories. The main departure point between the two is in the prediction of performance when a subject's arousal level is high on a well-learned task. In this situation, drive theory would predict that the quality of performance would be high, whereas the inverted 'U' theory would hypothesize a low performance. Rushall (1979: 56) made an interesting point when he stated that the more the elite athlete was aroused the better will be his performance. It is possible, he suggested, that elite athletes have learned to control their arousal to the extent that they never become too aroused (in the inverted 'U' sense). They only display the left hand side of the inverted 'U' curve.

AROUSAL AND ATTENTION

An understanding of the major concepts of the two theories outlined above are of considerable value in determining teaching strategies. However, in recent years there has been an increasing interest in the effect of arousal on attention. In an interesting approach to studying the arousal performance relationship, Easterbrook (1959) carried out a study of emotion and cue utilisation and suggested how performance deterioration may take place. He proposed that emotional arousal, such as fear of injury, acts consistently to reduce the range of cues a person utilises. Thus the gymnast is only able to concentrate on the most central cues. If these are the most relevant ones for good performance, such as maintaining the tuck position in the somersault, then he will be successful. However, he may attend to cues not relevant to successful performance, such as grasping the supporters arms, resulting in failure to complete the move.

The effect of arousal on attention has important implications for coaches. A high level of arousal will cause a narrowing of attention to what the performer thinks is most important. Accordingly, a coach must ensure that a performer is concentrating on the most relevant aspects for good performance. This may be a part of a move which a gymnast can perform successfully but needs improving technically, for example, the timing of the swing in the single leg upstart or the height of the legs in a cartwheel. On the other hand, the gymnast may be attempting a new move. This usually causes a high level of arousal with resultant narrowing of attention. In this case, the teacher should point out the most important aspect for successful performance, for example, placing the hands on the far end of the long horse in the straddle vault. Support should be given and initially the height and position of legs should be ignored. Only when the hands are automatically being placed correctly without conscious attention being given to this part of the move should the coach ask the gymnast to concentrate on improving other aspects. Accordingly, the aim is to develop correct responses which are made automatically. Moves should be over-learned so that they do not deteriorate under conditions which elicit high arousal such as competitions. In fact, the elite gymnast is often able to use this high arousal to his advantage as it is a source of energy which can provide more lift and flight in explosive moves. However, he also needs the emotional skill to calm down for moves best performed under lower conditions of arousal.

REGULATION OF AROUSAL

Changing arousal state in the desired direction requires an understanding of some of the basic principles of psychology such as those discussed above and skill in using certain techniques. The physical education teacher can achieve considerable success by applying these principles. Of particular importance is an understanding of factors which mediate the arousal-performance relationship and how they relate to the acquisition of gymnastic skills. Martens (1974) pointed out that task characteristics and individual differences are major considerations in seeking to determine the optimum arousal level for per-

formance of a particular task. Task characteristics of importance are (a) the amount of energy that must be expended to undertake the task, and (b) task difficulty.

It is not a simple matter, however, to analyse a task on these two dimensions and set about modifying the performer's arousal level for optimal performance. In order to analyse task difficulty in a meaningful way it is necessary to consider the stage of learning reached by the performer. One gymnast, for example, may consider the handspring a simple task, to another it may be very difficult. The expert may perform the skill best under conditions of relatively high arousal as it causes greater lift and flight. The novice however cannot tolerate a high level of arousal. As discussed above, this reduces the amount of information to which he can attend. As a result he is unable to attend to all the various coaching points necessary for him to successfully complete the move. The coach therefore should generally try to help the novice to practise with a medium level of arousal and concentrate on one specific aspect. The possible exception to this may be when the novice is making his first attempts at a difficult move requiring considerable muscular effort. In this instance a coach may need to 'gee up' the performer and encourage him to 'have a go'. Good support should be provided as the likelihood of success without support is often minimal. After the first attempt the initial fear is usually greatly reduced and the coach can then concentrate on regulating the performer's arousal level to the optimum for skilled performance.

With relation to task difficulty therefore a teacher must consider the stage the learner has reached in acquiring a particular skill as well as the complexity of the skill itself. In certain circumstances, such as practising linking moves or relatively simple moves involving balance and good timing, a coach may decide to concentrate on helping the gymnast work at an optimum arousal level. He may ask for less tension and encourage a smooth relaxed flow of movement. There are other moves however, which demand a high degree of arousal for successful performance. Most vaults and the explosive floor moves are included in this category. When he is teaching such a move a coach is faced with two alternatives. He can accept that the learner will be highly aroused and ask him to concentrate on one aspect only, since his capacity to attend to relevant information is severely reduced. An alternative approach is to create a situation where the performer is virtually carried through the move. With relatively low arousal and slow flight he will be able to attend to the various responses to be made throughout. Gradually the support may be reduced and the gymnast asked to produce more effort and speed. This approach is commonly used in the teaching of the flic-flac. The decision over which method to use should be made with an understanding of the principles involved. The nature of the skill should be analysed carefully. Consideration should also be given to the use of progressive practices since some gymnasts may prefer the wholistic method whereas others may prefer to learn stage by stage. Skills may be acquired more quickly if the appropriate method is adopted.

The teacher can have a considerable influence on a performer's arousal level by good use of verbal instructions. The voice and accompanying actions can motivate or demotivate performers quite dramatically. Accordingly, a teacher needs to develop a vocabulary of meaningful phrases such as 'punch out of the flic-flac' and 'drive the hips up'. When a gymnast is frightened, comments should be made which will reduce his fear and develop a feeling of confidence. The ability of a teacher or coach to instill a feeling of confidence is one of the most important aspects of good teaching.

In the preparation of teams for competition, a teacher or coach should bear in mind that the presence of an audience and the competitive situation will result in performers' arousal levels being higher than in training sessions. They should be warned of the effect this may have. Well learned moves, for example, may be performed with more lift and flight. Only well learned moves where the correct response is dominant should be included since the increased drive causes dominant responses to be produced. It is therefore necessary to 'over-learn' moves which are to be included in competition. Psychological preparation for competition can be of considerable value. A teacher or coach can carry this out by, for example, organising an individual competition among the team members or arranging for the gymnasts to practise in front of an audience.

In addition to regulating arousal to an appropriate level during the various learning stages, a teacher may use a variety of techniques to influence his gymnasts' motivation generally over long periods of time. Giving praise and reward can increase arousal but must only be given when correct responses are made. Realistic goals should be set so that a learner's level of aspiration and expectancy of success is at the appropriate level. If the task set is too hard the gymnast will quickly lose interest, if it is too easy he will soon become bored. Perhaps the single most important factor in maintaining motivation for participation and regulating that motivation to an optimal level is by ensuring that children experience success and enjoyment. Continual failure will rapidly cause a loss of interest resulting in boredom.

AROUSAL REGULATION TECHNIQUES WITH ELITE SPORTSMEN

The discussion so far has been aimed at helping teachers and club coaches to develop a deeper understanding of motivation and how the main concepts apply to practical situations. Coaches of elite gymnasts however should be made aware of the more sophisticated methods which may be used in the psychological preparation of his performers. It is beyond the scope of this book to examine these in detail, however some techniques are briefly mentioned below together with a number of references for coaches wishing to study arousal regulation in more depth. Siedentop (1978) outlined some of the problems which occur during the competitive season and suggests that many coaches simply resort to 'chiding and hassling stragglers'. This often results in tension between performers and coaches. A more efficient method, he argues, would be to employ behaviour management techniques. The technology of behaviour management is now sufficiently developed to be of practical use for teachers and coaches. It should be systematic and based on incentives rather than threats, on rewards rather than punishments. There is growing evidence, he says, that in sports settings it will prove to be every bit as powerful as it has in many other settings. It will increase performance while at the same time increasing performer and coach satisfaction. The primary system for managing the behaviour of gymnasts in practice settings is called 'contingency management' (a contingency is the relationship between a behaviour and a consequence). It is the management of these relationships that is important. The best system is one made up to fit the needs of a situation and should include consideration of aims, monitoring progress, and the most efficient reward system. In his article, Siedentop reported on a number of behaviour management studies which led to improved performance. All of them clearly show the importance of a definite strategy with intelligent use of rewards.

Siedentop's views on the need for a systematic method are shared by Fisher (1976:142) who cautioned coaches against an unorganized attack on performers' senses for the purpose of arousal. Instead of athletes being 'psyched up', he says, they will be 'psyched out'.

Behaviour management techniques are used mainly to produce a more general effect. They can have an important influence on arousal overall, but in order to regulate arousal at specific times coaches and performers can employ a variety of techniques. In recent years a considerable amount has been written on relaxation techniques. There are a variety that can be followed. Rushall (1979: 115) provides a detailed plan of relaxation training together with a training schedule. Transcendental meditation and hypnosis have also been used successfully to enhance sports performance.

These methods have the disadvantage of the coach not knowing if his performers are relaxed. As a result biofeedback techniques have been developed. This involves the use of instruments which record the physiological changes which occur as a person's arousal level changes. With an increase in arousal, a person's heart rate, blood pressure, breathing rate, muscular tension and skin conductance increases. These increases can be made evident to the performer either visually or by the use of a buzzer which changes in pitch. When the performer has information of his arousal level he can learn to regulate it by emotional control.

Systematic desensitization procedures developed by Wolpe (1974) may also be applied to improve sports performance. There are three aspects involved: training in deep muscle relaxation, construction of a list of anxiety producing situations in hierarchical order and relaxation paired with imagined anxiety provoking stimuli. A gymnast, for example, would first be taught muscle relaxation then asked to imagine the situations which cause him anxiety, such as the change of hand position on the high bar, while remaining relaxed. The mild anxiety which may arise is inhibited by the deep relaxation. This acts in the real situation by helping the gymnast experience less anxiety.

Once the relaxation technique has been learned and can be utilized, then it must be practised and actually incorporated into the gymnast's life style. It should be used when he is experiencing some frustration. This may occur when a move proves difficult to learn or a previously acquired skill is continually performed badly. The technique should always be used in practice sessions, otherwise they will be unlikely to work in competitive situations. A conscious effort must be made at the start of each routine, for example, to induce a calm controlled psychological state. Similarly, difficult moves must be approached with positive control over emotional arousal.

Techniques for overcoming emotional obstacles to learning and performance have also been developed in recent years. One which has met with some success is visual-motor behaviour rehearsal (Suinn 1972; Lane 1980). The gymnast must initially be made to relax. He is then asked to visualise the situation that is particularly stressful. Under this simulated stress situation, the gymnast can visualise himself successfully performing the skill or routine, ie coping with the situation. An example would be asking a person frightened by a large audience to visualise a crowd and then visualise himself stepping forward and executing his routine perfectly. In this example the performer may either mentally rehearse or actually practise while visualising an audience present.

A characteristic of top gymnasts is their ability to control their arousal levels prior to competition. They appear to inhibit anxiety reactions arising from participating in important competitions and control their attention to task orientated thoughts. The good coach is one who can help his performers achieve this emotional control. He should study the techniques he can use to raise and reduce arousal levels and develop an understanding of the psychological principles involved. In an earlier chapter the trend towards a more cognitive approach to understanding the learning process was discussed. In recent years there has also emerged a cognitive approach to motivation (Heckhaussen and Weiner 1972). There is evidence that emotion and subsequent actions are based on a person's cognitive evaluation of a situation. Emotions are a function of the individual's perception of his immediate stimulus situation. This has important implications for the coach. Performers may react very differently, for example, to situations which the coach may see as essentially similar, such as friendly competitions against another club. Similarly, a gymnast's anxiety over performing a new difficult move may fluctuate from one attempt to another. Accordingly, he will need to modify his techniques for helping the performer attain the optimum arousal level on each occasion.

Summary

Behaviour varies on two dimensions, direction and intensity. The direction of behaviour may be described as either moving toward or away from a stimulus situation. A person's behaviour, whether moving towards or away, will occur at a given intensity.

The study of motivation is an attempt to seek for causes of both dimensions of behaviour. One approach is to take a hedonistic viewpoint which contends that people engage in activities which will bring pleasure. Activities which are expected to have unpleasant outcomes are avoided.

Satisfying underlying needs and desires can bring pleasure. Accordingly, reasons why a person participates in gymnastics can be analysed in these terms. Sources of motivation and approach behaviour include the drive to satisfy the need for stimulation and activity, achievement, skill and excitement.

How a person interprets a set of stimuli or 'makes sense' of a situation is very important. If a person expects to be successful he will usually perform better. The value a person places on participation in gymnastics also strongly influences behaviour. 'Expectancy x value' theories stress the evaluation process that takes place as the individual subconsciously assesses the attractiveness of an activity as an outlet for his or her needs.

A person may be intrinsically or extrinsically motivated to participate in gymnastics (or both). If he participates because of intrinsic motivation, he does so because he finds participation rewarding. A person who is extrinsically motivated participates for external rewards such as prizes and badges.

Avoidance behaviour occurs when a person seeks to escape from a situation which he believes will lead to unpleasant outcomes. A child may participate in gymnastics through fear of reprimand from his teacher. Thus he is demonstrating avoidance behaviour. Once the external influence causing him to participate is removed he will cease to take part in gymnastics.

A gymnast is often in a conflict situation, having both a drive to approach a situation, eg, wanting to learn a new and difficult skill, and a drive to avoid the situation, eg, through fear of injury.

The intensity demension of motivated behaviour is referred to as arousal level. The arousal-performance relationship has received considerable attention. Two hypotheses have been put forward to explain this relationship, drive theory and the inverted 'U' hypothesis. The former suggests that performance is a product of habit and drive. With increased drive, dominant responses are made, which in the novice gymnast are incorrect ones, thus he makes an increased number of errors. The expert's performance may not deteriorate under high drive levels as his dominant responses are correct. Increased drive may in fact facilitate performance in the expert.

The inverted 'U' hypothesis proposes an optimum level of arousal for skilled performance. This level is mediated by a number of factors such as task difficulty and individual skill level.

Regulation of arousal level to optimum for the performance of a particular skill is an important part of teaching and coaching gymnastic skills.

Appendix A
Warm up and stretching activities

Warm-up games

There are many games which are suitable for use in the introductory section of a lesson. Outlined below is a selection of games suitable for use with most age groups. An inventive coach could devise many more.

Relays   On the whole relay games are not too successful in terms of body temperature raising activities as in the standard relay race most of the participants are waiting their turn most of the time. It is possible, however, to eliminate this 'waiting time' almost completely by using 'continuous' and sequential relays.

'CONTINUOUS' RELAY

The basic form is as follows: Each team stands on a line, evenly spaced out down the whole length of the gym. The team adopts the starting position, eg, sitting with legs stretched out at right angles to the line.

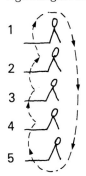

No. 1 stands and runs to the other end of the gym, jumping over the legs of his team mates. On reaching the other end of the gym No. 1 turns and runs back to his place but this time outside the line of the team, ie. he does not try to go back over their legs. On reaching his place he assumes the original starting position, ie sitting with legs outstretched. No. 2, who has been closely following number 1, jumps over No. 1's legs back into his place. No. 3, who has been closely following No. 2, jumps over the legs of No. 1, then No. 2 back into his place. This continues until the whole team has returned to its starting place.

Variations on the starting position:

(i)   Sitting in a tucked shape – team straddle jump over.
(ii) standing in straddle – team crawls through legs.
(iii) making a 'back' – team leap-frog over.
(iv) bridge position – team crawl under bridge.
(v)   standing to attention – team zigzags in and out.
(vi) combinations of the above.

SEQUENTIAL RELAY

The basic form is as follows: Teams of three or four form a single file behind a starting line as shown in diagram.

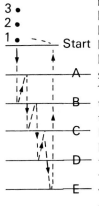

No. 1 runs to line B then back to line A, then to line C, back to line B, then to line D, back to line C . . . until, on reaching the last line, F, he runs back to his starting position. As soon as No. 1 has touched line A, No. 2 runs to line B (No. 1 is now on his way to line C). He now continues as No. 1, ie touching lines A, C, B, D, C . . . As soon as No. 2 has touched line A then No. 3 begins the sequence. This way the whole team is involved very quickly.

Variety could be introduced by, for example, stipulating that when going away from the starting line they run, when moving towards the starting line they hop. Other possibilities are obvious.

Another simple form of the relay is as follows: No. 1 runs to line A. He jumps backwards and forwards over the line, say, 6 times before running to line B and doing the same thing . . . etc. As soon as he leaves line A No. 2 starts. As soon as No. 2 moves to line B, No. 3 runs to line A. etc. This particular form of the relay is open to many variations. The participants can be asked to perform, say, 5 press-ups, sit-ups, burpees, or star jumps, etc at each line.

'PENALTY' OR 'CAPTURE' GAMES

These are probably the simplest of warm-up games to organise and involve the whole class immediately. The essence of the game is that any person who is 'caught' pays a penalty. The penalty could be to perform, say, ten press-ups or sit-ups, or to assume a position, for example a bridge, until released by a fellow player.

EXAMPLES

(i)   Class spreads out and each person sits cross-legged with hands on head. On command go everyone jumps up, touches all four walls and returns to places. Penalty awarded to last two or three to return to their starting positions.

(ii) Class runs freely in any direction. Teacher shouts out a number. Groups must quickly form, corresponding in size to the number called out, and sit down back to back. Penalty awarded to odd ones out or members of wrong sized groups.

(iii) Three or four people are selected to be 'on'. They are given a soft ball (a rolled up football sock is ideal), with which they try to hit any other player. Only those selected as 'on' are allowed to touch the ball. Penalty awarded to anyone else who is touched by the ball.

Note: It is good practice to change the 'catchers' frequently.

(iv) Two or three people are selected as 'on'. As soon as any other is 'caught' by being touched by any of those who are 'on', then he/she assumes a still position, say, standing with feet astride. Anyone who is 'caught' can only be set free again by someone who is already free crawling between their legs. Variations on this are leap-frog, crawling under a bridge . . . etc.

(v) One person is selected to be 'on'. As soon as he catches another by touching him, they must join hands and chase as a pair. This continues until there is a chain of four. The next one caught starts another chain. This continues until the winner is the last one to be caught.

Note: It is not advised to exceed the number of four in a chain. The 'whip-lash' effect on the last person in a long chain when the chain changes direction could have unfortunate consequences. With a little imagination a teacher could construct many similar games.

PARTNER ACTIVITIES

Again there are many games which can be played in two's or three's and add an extra element of fun to the end of a warm-up session. A few such games are illustrated below.

B tries to push A over

Rolling in a circle

Each tries to push the other over the line

Each tries to pull the other over the line

Standing and sitting as fast as possible

Each tries to put the other's shoulder on the floor

A lifts B up
B remains rigid

Stretching

There are six main areas for preparation:

(i) Ankles
(ii) Hamstrings
(iii) Hips
(iv) Spine
(v) Shoulders
(vi) Wrists

(i) ANKLES

(a) Sit on floor with legs straight and slightly apart. 'Draw' circles as big as possible with toes.
(b) In same position as above. Alternate pointing and lifting toes, ie extending and flexing of ankle joint through full range.
(c) Sitting on heels, toes pointed and feet together. Gently rock backwards and forwards lifting knees from floor (A)
(d) Skipping around the room pointing toes to the floor as hard as possible each time the foot is lifted (B)

A

B

C

(d) Stand close to wallbars. Keep legs straight, bend forwards and grasp bars about knee level. Keeping legs straight lean as far forwards from the bars as possible (D)

D

(iii) HIPS

(a) Squat with knees turned outwards. Alternately move right and left to straighten each leg in turn whilst keeping the hips as low as possible (A)
(b) Leg swinging sideways. Support leg must be kept straight and the foot flat on the floor. Each side 20 repetitions or more (B)

A

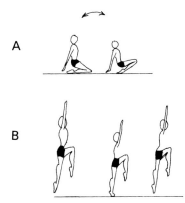

A

B

(ii) HAMSTRINGS

(a) Straddle stand. Keeping head well back and legs straight push backs of hands along the floor as far backwards as possible (A)
(b) Stand with feet together, legs bent and hands flat on floor. Maintaining the flat hand contact with the floor rhythmically bend and straighten the legs. Placing the hands further back will make the exercise more demanding (B)
(c) Straddle sitting with toes pointed. Alternately touch left foot with right hand and then *vice versa*. Try to get chest to knee (C)

B

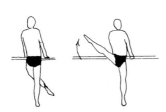

G

(c) From straddle stand gradually work the legs further and further apart until it is not possible to straddle wider. Stretch arms forwards and gently sit without allowing the hands to touch the floor. Try to regain straddle stand position by 'swimming' arms and shoulders forwards.

(d) Lying on back in straddle position, hold on to the heels and firmly and gently pull feet down towards the floor (D)

(e) Sitting in straddle facing the wallbars with the seat touching the bars firmly pull the chest towards the bars (E)

(iv) SPINE

Great care must be taken when exercising this area of the body especially with young children whose bones are still developing and soft. In general this region should be exercised to maintain the mobility which is already there. Attempting to increase natural mobility could be dangerous.

(a) 'Happy cat – Angry cat' These shapes are fundamental in gymnastics and should be practiced often (A)

(b) 'Rocking horse' (B)

D

A

E

B

C

(c) Tuck up as tightly as possible ensuring that the back is well rounded. Take arms behind the head then arch the back (C)

(d) From a handstand arch back and fall to bridge (D). From bridge position bend the legs and jump back through handstand.

(f) Take up a very low lunge position. Push hips rhythmically towards the floor whilst pulling the shoulders backwards. (Important: It is vital that the feet should be kept in line. The back foot should not be turned out at right angles) (F)

(g) Kneel down sitting back on the heels and grasping the ankles. Stretch up and push the hips as far forwards as possible (G)

D

F

E

(e) Straddle stand with trunk horizontal. Alternately point left then right hand towards the ceiling ensure a good twist of the spine (E)

(f) Straddle stand with feet shoulder width apart. Circle hips in as big a circle as possible ensuring a hollowing of the spine as the hips are circled to the front and a rounding of the spine when they are circled to the back.

(g) 1 Straddle sit and, gently but firmly, slowly nod the head forwards and backwards to the limit of mobility.

2 Turn the head right and left to limit of movement.

3 Combining 1 and 2 roll the head round in as big a circle as possible.

4 Finally relax the neck muscles and loosely roll the head round.

(v) SHOULDERS

(a) Holding a towel or stick, keep the arms straight and parallel and pass the stick backwards over the head. Without releasing the stick pass it back over the head again to the front. This should be done with the hands as close as possible but without the necessity to bend the arms (A)

(b) Partners place hands on each others shoulders keeping the arms straight. Each gently and rhythmically pushes the others chest towards the floor (B)

A

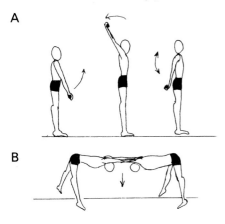

B

(c) Arm circling both ways brushing the ears with the arms on every circle.

(d) From the front support position lift the hips as high as possible then push the head between the arms to try and touch nose to knees.

D

(e) Hands on support (wallbars or box). Keeping arms straight push the chest towards the floor (E)

E

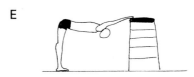

(f) Sitting on the floor with hands pointing backwards push the seat along the floor and relax to get the back as flat on the floor as possible. Arms should remain shoulder width apart (F)

F

(g) Back hanging from wallbars or bar (G)

(h) Handstand against a wall. Push the head through the arms and the seat towards the wall. Move the shoulders as far from the wall as possible.

Note: This exercise is for the more able gymnast (H)

G

H

The following exercises are for the older children. The partner's role is to 'help not injure' and this point should be stressed.

(i) Sitting on floor with arms back partner keeps arms shoulder width apart and gently lifts the arms upwards (I)

(j) Partners sit back to back with arms in air holding each others wrists. One partner bends forwards and pulls the others hands as close to the floor as possible. Action is then repeated by other partner.

Note: This exercise may also be used for hamstring stretching especially if the partner bending forwards does so with feet apart and legs straight.

(k) One gymnast assumes a bridge shape whilst holding the heels of his partner. Partner grasps under shoulders and gently pulls shoulders upwards and backwards (K)

(c) As above (b) with fingers pointing sideways. Shoulders are moved to the right and left with the heels of the hands maintaining contact with the floor (B)

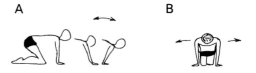

A   B

(d) 'Sea lion'. Take up a front support position. Keeping legs straight and together walk forwards on the hands dragging the feet on the floor behind.

I

J

K

(iv) WRISTS

Whilst it is doubtful if mobility can be improved in this area of the body to any significant degree it is important that the joint be stretched especially prior to activities which require the body weight to be taken on the hands.

(a) Relax wrists and shake them up and down, then shake them side to side.

(b) Kneel down placing hands flat on floor with fingers pointing forwards. Keeping the heels of the hands on the floor gently rock the shoulders forwards and backwards over the hands (A)

Appendix B
The judging and organisation of schools competitions

Judging a gymnastic performance according to the rules of the Federation Internationale de Gymnastique (FIG) Code of Points is a very complicated matter requiring a great deal of experience. Indeed, the complexity of this method may well deter teachers of gymnastics from organising and running gymnastic competitions. The aim of this section is to allay any fears which teachers may have concerning judging, firstly by outlining two easy methods of judging and secondly by explaining, in a simplified manner, the basic concepts on which more complex systems of judging are based.

Method A

Perhaps the simplest form of judging is a 'knock-out' type of competition. Here the judge(s) must see two performances and merely say which one is considered to be the best – the first or the second. He need not say by how much as no numerical value, in terms of a score, is asked for. Indeed, a panel containing an odd number of judges will always give a decision. This type of competition has been used in some branches of gymnastics, eg, tumbling contests, and has a great spectator appeal. Unfortunately, unless the demands made upon the gymnast, in terms of length of sequence, is minimal, and there are only a few competitors, this method is quite unsuitable. In any eventuality the winner of such a competition would have to perform his sequence several times over. It is also worth considering that whilst this is a very simple way to judge two performances, as no assessment has to be made concerning the value of each sequence performed, the problem of why one sequence is better than another has not been discussed. As soon as one begins to explore this question then the method, so far considered simple, suddenly appears much more complex.

Method B

As already mentioned, no numerical value need be put on sequences judged on a simple knock-out format where one performance is compared directly with one other on a win or lose basis. A judging system which requires somewhat more experience, yet is simple enough to be used in elementary competition, is one in which the 'standard' against which the following routines are judged is set by the first performer.

Following the first performance the judges meet and discuss the sequence, finally awarding a score. Subsequent competitors receive scores higher or lower than the 'set' score depending upon the degree by which the subsequent sequences are better or worse. This technique is often used but is rather subjective and consequently somewhat 'rough and ready'.

A more complex system of judging

Most gymnastic performances are judged according to two factors:
1 The rules of competition.
2 A comparison made by the judge between the actual performance witnessed and the judge's own conception of the perfect performance.

The 'perfect' form of a skill is agreed by concensus. For example, the perfect handspring would have straight legs, straight arms, lift from the hands, correct body shape in flight, etc. A judge would then compare the performance which is offered with his own concept of the perfect move. Marks would then be lost depending upon the degree of deviance demonstrated by the performer from the concept of the perfect move performance.

In an attempt to be as objective in assessment as possible, sets of rules are drawn up which have two functions:
1 To describe the 'perfect' performance.
2 To fix the penalties which are to be applied to the various deviations which may be demonstrated in an actual performance.

This is most clearly illustrated with regard to vaulting.

The vault which is to be performed is described, usually in picture form, with other requirements stated, eg, the vaulter's hips must reach a certain height – say one metre – above the height of the horse, the landing must be made at least two metres from the horse, etc.

The vault is given a tariff. This is the mark/score which would be awarded to the vaulter if he performed the vault perfectly. This tariff usually reflects the difficulty of the vault so that simple vaults, eg, through vault, straddle vault, would be allotted a lower tariff than more difficult vaults, eg, handspring, cartwheel.

Thus the gymnast starts off with the tariff mark, say 10.00. All the possible faults are listed and the size of the deduction which the judge may make from the basic score, ie, the tariff is given. An example of part of a typical list is given below.

Fault	Deduction	
Failure to reach minimum height in flight	- 0.1 - 0.5	(This means that the judge may deduct between 0.1 and 0.5 points from the basic score depending on how much the gymnasts performance deviated from that required.)
Poor form in execution, ie, bending of arms or legs or poor positioning of limbs	- each time 0.1 - 0.3	
Poor body shape during vault	- 0.1 - 0.5	
Unsteady landing	- 0.1 - 0.3	
Failure to show good flight from horse, ie, landing less than two metres from horse	- 0.1 - 0.5	

When the gymnast has performed his vault the judge totals all the tenths of points which he has taxed the performance according to the judging code, ie, the list above. This total taxation is deducted from the tariff and what is left constitutes the gymnasts score for that particular performance.

The judging of a sequence is somewhat more complicated but, nevertheless follows the same principle. For convenience, and to help in the objectivity of the judging process, the sequence is considered under a number of headings:

1   DIFFICULTY

This aspect may or may not appear depending upon the level of the competition. Basically the organiser(s) state how many skills from different difficulty categories are required for full 'difficulty' marks. The skills would be listed in difficulty categories. If the required number of skills of particular difficulty were not demonstrated in the sequence then the gymnast would lose points accordingly. A careful study of the two examples of a competition format which follow illustrate this clearly. Example 1 has no 'difficulty' requirements whilst Example 2 does.

2   COMBINATION

This deals with how the sequence is constructed. Again rules are laid down and points deducted according to the deviation from these rules. A sequence demonstrating only eight elements where ten were required will be penalised for the lack of two missing elements at a rate laid down by the competition organiser(s). Similarly, various types of skill may be asked for, eg, a balance, spring, roll, jump, etc, when examples of these types of skill are not shown the gymnast would be penalised. Apart from these more tangible requirements other aspects of a performance may also be demanded, eg, changes of pace, changes of levels, fluency of movement, etc. Again a performance may be taxed according to the rules if these aspects are not evident.

3   FORM IN EXECUTION

Each time the gymnast performs a skill with form faults, eg, bent arms, bent legs, poor body shape, poor control, etc, then he is penalised according to the rules.

Following a sequence performance the judge totals up all the points which he has deducted under the headings outlined above. This total is then deducted from the starting mark of 10.00 points. What remains is the gymnast's score for that performance.

The more complex competition, the more complex the rules and thus the more experience is required of the judges.

A consideration of this short discussion of judging theory clearly throws into relief certain implications for any competition organiser.

Firstly the competition requirements must be tailored to suit the competitors. If the competition is aimed, say, a very basic level then the rules should be as simple as possible and the requirements minimal, consistent, of course, with the spirit of the competition.

Secondly, if any degree of objectivity is to be demonstrated by the judges then the experience of the judges is most important. It would be self-defeating for example, to publish a long list of judging rules for a simple school competition where judges are usually inexperienced. Such a situation would result in enormous feats of mental gymnastics being performed by the judges completely out of keeping with the levels of performance demonstrated by gymnasts themselves. It would be well for organisers of this basic level to keep in mind that the more numerous the opportunities which exist when individual judges have to make a decision, then the more likely it is that the final marks awarded by different judges for the same sequence will be at variance.

Thirdly, however the rules are stated in order to give an as objective an assessment of the value of a performance as possible, there will always be differences of opinion. Whilst it is possible to state exactly *what* is to be done, *how* well the skill has been performed can not be stated exactly. Even very experienced judges who have seen and assessed many thousands of gymnastic performances may, and probably do, have different concepts of perfection for each skill. As the worth of each skill is assessed in comparison with the individual concept of perfection then, clearly, there is likely to be little individual variance. Multiply the little variances by the number of times that similar decisions have to be made during the performance of a sequence and variations in scores awarded for the same sequence can be understood.

Much of the above will become clearer if a careful study is made of the two examples of possible competition formats.

The organisation of a school gymnastic competition

The details of organisation will vary depending upon such factors as the level of competition (eg, inter-form, school individual, inter-school, area, region, etc), the number of competitors/teams, the number and types of group (eg, under 13 boys, over 13 boys, etc), the number and experience of judges, etc. As a consequence the smaller details can only be finalised by the competition organiser to suit the competition he is organising.

There are however, certain common elements which will be discussed. The first consideration must be personal. These can be listed as follows:

1   COMPETITION ORGANISER

This person has overall responsibility. He must organise dates, venue, equipment and personnel (details of individual duties are given below).

2   COMPETITION CONTROLLER

The competition controller's job is to ensure that the competition runs smoothly. He must ensure that competitors know where to wait for their turns to perform, where the judges sit, inform the marshals of their duties, etc. The competition controller often doubles as the announcer, which is important because a good announcer can do a great deal to ensure that there are few hold-ups and that the competition is kept moving.

3   JUDGES

Judges should understand the judging basis of the competition and be experienced enough to judge an individual performance accurately, quickly and fairly. Inexperienced judges often take a long time to reach a decision which holds up the competition and in turn prolongs the waiting time for the competitors. For an internal school competition it is often possible to invite an experienced judge to the school competition and manage with only one respected judge. (This is not the case, obviously if large numbers of children are involved.) Failing this two judges, whose marks are averaged, is a recommended procedure. For inter-school competitions it is advisable to invite an independent master judge into the panel. Quite often the person judging a home or away team will be the most gymnastically experienced person on the staff. Invariably this is the person who trained the gymnasts and consequently there is often an unconscious bias towards their own gymnasts which becomes reflected in the marks awarded. An independent judge can even out this tendency.

4   SCORER AND RUNNERS

The competition organiser will supply the scorer with a master score sheet. On this sheet will be entered the marks gained by each competitor. A runner will normally sit by a judge and take the slip of paper (judges slip!), bearing the competition mark to the scorer. Where two or more judges are concerned with the same competitor either one of the judges, designated as master judge, will average the marks given and send a single slip to the score table, or the runner will take all the slips to the score table for the scorer to average. In a large competition it often saves much confusion at the scorer's table if only one slip clearly marked with the competitors name/number, section and score is received.

5   COMPETITION MARSHALS

If the competition is to run smoothly and with the minimum waste of time it is important that each competitor is ready to perform when called upon by the judge(s). To achieve this a marshal is needed for each group of competitors. He will have a list of the competitors in his group and the order in which they are to compete. (This should tally with the order given to the judges by the organiser).

6 TIMEKEEPER

When warm ups and/or routines have to be timed then a timekeeper will be required. Performers who exceed the time allocated must be reported to the master judge. It is common for the timekeeper to sit by the judge in order that this information can be given without delay following the completion of a performance.

The six jobs mentioned above are basic to a gymnastic competition, but the list can be added to depending upon the size and status of the competition. A large school, or inter-school match in which two, three or more schools are taking part would mean several groups working at the same time. This would require more judges, scorers, marshals and timekeepers. Doubling up of jobs may not be possible and a full complement of officials may well be required. The converse is also true however. At a small school competition to which one of the authors was invited to officiate the duties of judge, scorer, and announcer were taken on! As a general rule, however, it is advisable to have one person to each job wherever possible.

However small or large the competition its successful running will depend upon good preplanning by the organiser. Below is a list, with items placed in chronological order, of the tasks which need to be completed by the organiser. No indication is given as to the time scale as this will depend on the size and complexity of the competition, availability of suitable officials, ages of competitors, etc.

1 Establish and publish the details of the competition, ie, format, date, judging basis.
2 Approach and appoint suitable officials.
3 Ensure that judges have a copy of the judging format in time to familiarise themselves with it.
4 Receive entries by a specified date which must be notified with the original publicity material.
5 Sort out the entries to coincide with the published groupings, eg, under 13 boys, over 11

girls, etc.
6 Make a 'draw' with each group of entries to establish the working order of the gymnasts.
7 Publish the groupings and competition order.
8 Send the officials details of the competition. (To remind them of their promised commitment!)
9 Brief competition controller on details of competition and supply with sufficient lists of competitors and order of competition for marshals.
10 Supply sufficient judging slips.
11 Supply master score sheet(s).
12 Supply prizes.
13 Ensure that the announcer knows who to thank in his final address before announcing the winners.
14 Remember to *thank all helpers personally*.
15 Publish and distribute the results.
16 Make a list of successes/problems and other details of organisation which will help the organisation of next years competition.

Competition programme

It is only possible to speak in general terms under this heading again, as the competition programme will vary depending upon all the variables of size, status, etc, mentioned under previous headings. It would be of some value, however, to offer an outline programme and add some comments under various sections.

OUTLINE COMPETITION PROGRAMME

Time Start of pre-competition warm-up.
The length of time allocated to the precompetition warm-up should be great enough for each gymnast to suitably be warmed up but not too long as a long warm-up period often turns into a training session!

Time End of warm-up – gymnasts leave the competition area and prepare to march on.

Time March on and presentation of gymnasts.
A march on of competitors, however big or small the competition/audience is a valuable exercise as it can,
(a) announce the start of the competition
(b) give a sense of occasion to the gymnasts.

Time March off to first event(s) and begin competition warm-up.

It is customary to allow a short warm-up period (2 or 3 minutes) at the commencement of each round or event. This period must be timed and general use of the apparatus must terminate strictly at the end of this time. As soon as the competition controller/announcer call the end of this warm-up time the marshal(s) should ensure that the first gymnast(s) is/are ready to perform.

In a school competition the organiser may feel that another warm-up immediately prior to the start of the first event could be dispenced with. A short warm-up before subsequent rounds/events should be allowed as the gymnasts will inevitably have spent a large proportion of competition time sitting down waiting to perform.

The groups should, ideally, consist of no more than eight gymnasts. Groups of larger sizes will necessitate long periods of waiting for gymnasts and would ensure a long, drawn out competition which would not be conductive to good performances.

In a competition with say, two events, as in the example previously given requiring each gymnast to perform a floor routine and an apparatus routine, it would be desirable to have two groups, A and B. Whilst A performs on the floor routine, group B performs the apparatus routine. In round two they simply change over. The judges, however, do not change with the groups but remain to judge the second group on the same event. This is of course, to ensure a degree of consistency.

When the number of gymnasts exceeds the suggested group size of eight, then it is suggested that 4 groups be formed, not 3. We now have groups A, B, C and D. Groups A and B would work as already described and then groups C and D would repeat the process. This is far superior than having each group perform on one event and then wait through a whole round before competing on the second.

Whilst the overall time of the competition would be unaffected the waiting time between performances for individual gymnast would be kept to a minimum. The number of groups, then should increase as multiples of the number of routines required from each individual gymnast.

It is important to re-state that all competitors in any competition class, eg, boys under 13 Floor, girls under 11 Apparatus, etc, be judged by the same judge(s). With the best will in the world a judge taking over a competition class from another judge would find great difficulty judging to the same standard. At the end of this round the gymnasts should be lined up and march to the marshalling point for the next round. Again this may appear something of a 'frill' but does help add to the sense of occassion for the gymnasts as well as marking the end of the round for spectators.

Time Warm-up for round 2 – start of round 2.

The end of the warm-up period should be called and then round 2 proper will begin. This will continue to its conclusion as round 1.

Time Gymnasts from groups A and B march off and groups C and D march on to their first event.

This is assuming of course, that there are four groups. Rounds 3 and 4 continue as rounds 1 and 2. Assuming that there are no other groups, groups C and D now march off at the termination of round 4. This procedure will announce the end of the competition.

Time March on and presentation of prizes.

All gymnasts march on and line up. Results are read and prizes presented before gymnasts once again march off. This final march off will mark the termination of the entire proceedings.

Further organisational note: Where large numbers of gymnasts are involved and/or when the amount of apparatus available is limited, it is possible to use a doubling up system. This technique can be explained in the following example: Two groups are to perform say, on the floor, a group of 8 boys and a group of girls. A girl completes her routine first. While the judge(s) consider(s) the mark to be awarded, the first boy performs his routine which will be marked of course by a different judge(s). This alternating of performers allows the overall competition time to be reduced but does require more judges. Using this system two pieces of apparatus can be used by four groups.

Examples of competition formats

Two examples are offered. The first is a competition which could be used as a basis for a school championship or an inter-school competition on a local basis. It is based on the approach to teaching gymnastics suggested in this book. The second example is an actual competition designed for use on a national scale by the English Schools Gymnastics Association (ESGA).

Example 1

THE SCHOOL GYMNASTIC CHAMPIONSHIP

Format:

Age groups:
Boys and Girls under 13 years – Junior Championship
Boys and Girls over 13 years – Senior Championship

REQUIREMENTS

Each competitor will be required to perform two routines:

1 A floor routine
2 An apparatus routine.

1 FLOOR ROUTINE

The routine is to consist of 10 recognisable core skills and/or variations lasting a maximum of 40 seconds with the skills linked together by suitable simple movements to produce a fluent routine. The routine should show elements which include a jump, roll, balance and a turn as well as demonstrating the use of different levels, speeds and dynamics.

2 APPARATUS ROUTINE

The apparatus layout shown below must be used. The routine must consist of 8 *core skills* and/or *variations* (see Chapter 2), at least one element being shown on each piece of apparatus. A maximum time limit is 40 seconds in which a fluent routine demonstrating a variety of types of skill is to be preferred.

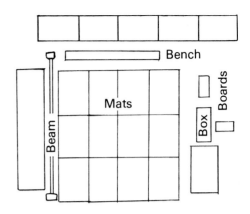

JUDGING BASIS

1 FLOOR ROUTINE

The gymnast will start off with 10.00 points from which deductions will be made according to the following table.

(a) For each missing skill
from the required 10 . . . 0.5 per skill

(b) Failure to show a jump,
roll, balance and turn . . . 0.3 per missing type of skill

(c) Poor use of different levels, speeds, and dynamics (routine construction) . . . up to 1.00

(d) Poor form and technique (execution*) . . . up to 4.00

(e) For each second over 40 second limit total mark allocation: . . . 0.1

elements	5.00 (ten elements at 0.5)
execution	4.00
construction	1.00
total	10.00

2 APPARATUS ROUTINE

The gymnast will start with 10.00 points from which deductions will be made according to the following table.

(a) Failure to use 8 skills . . . 0.5 per missing and/or variations   skill

*See page 129

(b) Failure to use each ... 1.00 per apparatus
piece of apparatus
(ie, box, beam and
bench)

(c) Poor construction of ... up to 1.0
routine, ie, different
types of skills, speed,
levels, etc, not shown

(d) Poor form and ... up to 5.00
technique (execution)

(e) For each second over ... 0.1
40 second time limit

total mark allocation:		
	elements	4.00
	execution	5.00
	construction	1.00
	total	10.00

Execution:
Where poor form or technique is demonstrated and deduction of between 0.1 and 0.3 points should be made depending upon the degree of deviation from correct form. Examples of poor form are: arms or legs bent (when not required by the skill), poor head position, excess bending forward or backward of the body. At the end of the routine all the deduction made under this heading are added together and the total deducted from the allocation of marks for this aspect.

General notes
Ideally each performance should be judged by two judges whose marks would be averaged. In inter-school competitions a third judge, preferably independent and neutral is desirable. Unlike the following example of a competition format (that designed on behalf of the ESGA) no direct account has been taken concerning the difficulty of the elements included in the routines. This has been done deliberately as the authors consider that quality of movement should be the dominating factor rather than complexity. Also the competition would be further complicated for the judges who have to recognise skills and their variations as belonging to *'difficulty'* categories (in more complex competitions moves are actually graded according to difficulty ... see Example 2 below. Teachers, however, who are sufficiently experienced to cater for the more complex requirements of such a competition may wish to construct one along similar lines to Example 2 below.

Example 2

Format:

Team and Age Group:
a team consists of 5 members with the best 4 scores on floor and vault to count towards the final team total. All members of the team to be over 13 years of age in the school year of the competition, (ie, 13 on 1 September)

Floor:
A sequence to be performed on an area not to exceed 12 metres square. (Mats to be placed where required within the limitation.)

Time Limits:
The sequence is to last between 35 and 45 seconds. Music is optional for Boys and Girls. Penalty 0.1 marks per second over or under time.

Requirements:
At least one move from group one plus four moves from group two should be performed for maximum difficulty marks.

Group 1	Group 2
Forward somersault	Flic-flac
Backward somersault	Handspring
Free cartweel	Flyspring
Two or more con-	Jump with full turn
secutive flic-flacs	Split leap
Handstand full	Dive roll
pirouette	Handstand (3 seconds)
	Single pirouette on one foot
	Forward walkover
	Backward walkover
	One hand cartweel (2nd hand)
	Backward roll to handstand (momentary)
	Headspring

The moves are to be linked together to form a fluent sequence which shows good use of the available floor area and a balanced distribution of the required elements. The sequence should include jumps, rolls, turns, step combinations, balances and supple moves to link the agilities together harmoniously.

Marking:
The sequence is to be marked out of ten as follows:

Difficulty   3.00
Execution   4.00
Composition 3.00

Marks will be deducted for lack of content, ie, 1.00 for each required move missing from group one, and 0.5 for each required move missing from group two, poor form and incorrect technique in execution, insufficient variety of moves, poor use of floor area available, lack of flow, rhythm and harmony, too short or too long a routine.

Vaulting:
Each competitor will have two vaults (ie, two attempts) and the best score will count. The vault will take place over a type 'A' box (approx 3 ft 4 in. high) using a springboard or reuther board. A safe landing must be provided. The box can be used either long or cross ways. (NB generally speaking a long box will show a vault with greater amplitude than the same vault performed on a cross box.)

Marking:
Vaults will be judged according to the following tariff list:

Squat vault (through vault) with bent legs	– 8.50
Straddle vault	– 8.50
Squat vault (through vault) legs straight	– 9.50
Handspring vault	– 10.00

Breadown for judging:

Fault		Maximum deduction
First flight on	up to	2.00
Thrust and flight off	up to	2.00
Form and Shape of vault	up to	3.00
Landing	up to	1.00

REFERENCES

Adams, J.A., 'A closed loop theory of motor behaviour', *Journal of Motor Behaviour*, 1971, 3, 111–149

Alderman, R.B., 'Incentive motivation in sport: An interpretive speculation of research opportunities', in A. Craig Fisher (ed), *Psychology of Sport*, Palo Alto: Mayfield, 1976

Anderson, J.R., *Cognitive Psychology and Its Implications*, San Francisco: W.H. Freeman, 1980

Bandura, A. *Aggression: A Social Learning Analysis*, Englewood Cliffs: Prentice Hall, 1973

Beck, R.C. *Motivation: Theories and Principles*, New Jersey: Prentice Hall, 1978

Berlyne, D., *Conflict, Curiosity and Arousal*, New York: McGraw-Hill, 1960

Bilbrough, A. and Jones, P., *Physical Education in the Primary School*, London: University of London Press, 1963

Bilbrough, A. and Jones, P., *Developing Patterns in Physical Education*, London: University of London Press, 1973

Brame, J.M., 'The effects of expectancy and previous task cues on motor performance, *Journal of Motor Behaviour*, 1979, Vol. 11, No. 3, 215–223

Cratty, B., *Movement Behaviour and Motor Learning* (3rd ed), Philadelphia: Lea and Febiger, 1975

Deci, E.L., *Intrinsic Motivation*, New York: Plenum Press, 1975

Duffy, E., 'The psychological significance of the concept of arousal or activation', *Psychological Review*, 1957, Vol. 64, No. 5, 265–275

Easterbrook, J.A., 'The effect of emotion on cue utilisation', *Psychological Review*, 1959, 66, 153–201

Fisher, A.C., *Psychology of Sport*, Palo Alto: Mayfield, 1976

Fitts, P. and Posner, M., *Human Performance*, London: Prentice Hall, 1973

Fleishman, E.A., *The Structure and Measurement of Physical Fitness*, Englewood Cliffs, New York: Prentice Hall, 1964

Gentile, A.M., 'A working model of skill acquisition with application to teaching', *Quest, Monograph Series*, 1972, 17, 3–23

Gray, J.A., *The Psychology of Fear and Stress.* London: Weidenfield and Nicholson, 1971

Harvey, N., and Greer, K., 'Actions: the mechanisms of motor control', in G. Claxton (ed), *Cognitive Psychology: New Directions*, London: Routledge and Kegan Paul, 1980

Heckhausen, H. and Weiner, B., 'The emergence of a cognitive psychology of motivation', in P.C. Dodwell (ed), *New Horizons in Psychology (2)*, London: Penguin, 1972

Hilgard, E., Atkinson, R. and Atkinson, R., *Introduction to Psychology* (5th ed), New York: Harcourt, Brace and Janovich, 1971

Hill, W.F., 'Activity as an autonomous drive', *Journal of Comparative Physiological Psychology*, 1956, 49, 15–19

Jackson, D.N., Ahmed, S.A. and Heapy, N.A., 'Is achievement a unitary construct?', *Journal of Research in Personality*, 1976, 10, 1–21

Kagan, J. and Berkun, M., 'The reward value of running activity', *Journal of Comparative Physiological Psychology*, 1954, 47, 108

Knapp, B., *Skill in Sport*, London: Routledge Kegan Paul, 1963

Landers, D., 'The arousal-performance relationship revisited', *Research Quarterly for Exercise and Sport*, 1980, Vol. 51, No. 1, 77–90

Lane, J.F., 'Improving athletic performance through visuo-motor behaviour rehearsal', in R. Suinn (ed), *Psychology of Sports: Methods and Applications*, Minneapolis: Burgess, 1980

Lindsay, P.H. and Norman, D.A., *Human Information Processing*, New York: Academic Press, 1977

Lockhart, A., 'Communicating with the learner', *Quest, Monograph Series*, 1966, No. 6, 57–67

Low, D., 'Information processing in the highly skilled sports situation', *Momentum* (UK), 1978, Vol. 3, No. 3, 11–18

Mahoney, M.J., *Cognition and Behaviour Modification*, Cambridge (Mass.): Ballinger, 1974

Martens, R., 'Arousal and motor performance', in J.H. Wilmore (ed), *Exercise and Sports Science Reviews (Vol 2)*, New York: Academic Press, 1974

Massimo, J., 'Motivation in gymnastics: A key to success', *International Gymnast*, 1976, No. 10, October, 58

Maulden, B. and Layson, J., *Teaching Gymnastics* (2nd ed), London: MacDonald and Evans, 1979

Medcof, J. and Roth, J., *Approaches to Psychology*, Milton Keynes: Open University Press, 1979

Miller, R.B., 'Task taxonomy: Science or technology?', *Ergonomics*, 1967, 10, 167–176

Murray, M.J., 'Matching cognitive mode with teaching methodology in learning a move motor skill', *Research Quarterly*, 1979, Vol. 50, No. 1, 80–87

Neisser, U., *Cognitive Psychology*, New York: Appleton Century Crofts, 1967

Rushall, B., *Psyching in Sport: The Psychological Preparation for Serious Competition in Sport*, London: Pelham, 1979

Rushall, B. and Siedentop, D., *The Development and Control of Behaviour in Sport and Physical Education*, Philadelphia: Lea and Febiger 1972

Sage, G.H., *Introduction to Motor Behaviour: A Neuropsychological Approach* (2nd ed), Reading: (Mass.) Adison-Wesley, 1977

Schmidt, R.A., 'A schema theory of discrete motor skill learning', *Psychological Review*, 1975, 82 225–260

Selder, D.J. and Del Rolan, 'Knowledge of performance, skill level and performance on the balance beam', *Canadian Journal of Applied Sport Sciences*, 1979, 4(3), 226–229

Siedentop, D., 'The management of practice behaviour', in W.F. Straub (ed), *Sport Psychology: An Analysis of Athlete Behaviour*, New York: Mouvement Publications, 1978

Singer, R., *Motor Learning and Human Performance* (2nd ed), New York: Macmillan Publishing Co Inc, 1975

Straub, W.F. (ed), *Sport Psychology: An Analysis of Athlete Behaviour*, New York: Mouvement Publications, 1978

Suinn, R.M., 'Removing emotional obstacles to learning and performance by visuo-motor behaviour rehearsal', *Behaviour Therapy*, 1972, 3, 308–310

Wallace, J. and Hagler, R., 'Knowledge of performance and the learning of a closed motor skill', *Research Quarterly*, 1979, 50, No. 2, 265–271

Weiner, B., *Theories of Motivation: From Mechanism to Cognition*, Chicago: Markham, 1972

Welford, A.T., *Fundamentals of Skill*, London: Methuen, 1968

Welford, A.T., *Skilled Performance: Perceptual and Motor Skills*, Glenview (Illinois): Scott Foresman, 1976

White, R.W., Motivation reconsidered: The concept of competence, *Psychological Review*, 1959, 66, 5, 297–333

Whiting, A.T.A., *Concepts in Skill Learning*, London: Lepus Books, 1975

Willee, A.W., 'Directive and non-directive teaching methods', *FIEP Bulletin*, 1978, Vol. 48, No. 4. 13–29

Wolpe, J., *The Practice of Behaviour Therapy* (2nd ed), New York: Maxwell House, 1974

INDEX

DATE	
APR 0 8 1985	NOV 1 1 1987
APR 2 2 1985	MAR 2 0 1988
DEC 0 7 1985	DEC 1 0 1992
JAN 2 7 1986	APR 2 5 1997
APR 0 1 1986	APR 2 5 1997
	DEC 2 3 1997
APR 2 0 1986	DEC 1 0 1997
NOV 0 6 1986	DEC 0 6 2001
FEB 1 2 1987	NOV 2 9 2001
MAR 0 4 1988	MAY 1 5 2003

APR 1 1 2003

FEB 2 3 2005

NOV 1 0 2005

APR 1 6 2007

APR 1 7 2007